1500

Late-Twentieth-Century Skyscrapers

Late-Twentieth-Century
SKYSCRAPERS

Piera Scuri

VNR VAN NOSTRAND REINHOLD
_____ New York

Copyright © 1990 by Van Nostrand Reinhold

Library of Congress Catalog Card Number 89-37158
ISBN 0-442-23789-8

Printed in the United States of America

Van Nostrand Reinhold
115 Fifth Avenue
New York, New York 10003

Van Nostrand Reinhold International Company Limited
11 New Fetter Lane
London EC4P 4EE, England

Van Nostrand Reinhold
480 La Trobe Street
Melbourne, Victoria 3000, Australia

Nelson Canada
1120 Birchmount Road
Scarborough, Ontario M1K 5G4, Canada

16 15 14 13 12 11 10 9 8 7 6 5 4 3 2 1

Library of Congress Cataloging-in-Publication Data

Scuri, Piera.
    Late-twentieth-century skyscrapers/Piera Scuri.
        p.   cm.
    ISBN 0-442-23789-8
    1. Skyscrapers—United States.   2. Architecture, Postmodern-
United States.   I. Title.   II. Title: Late 20th century
skyscrapers.
NA6232.S27   1990
720′.483′097309047—dc20   89-37158
                                                              CIP

To Douglas

Contents

Preface

If we begin with the assumption that churches are the expression
of religious power and castles of aristocratic power, and that architecture is the expression of the society that creates it, then it follows
that skyscrapers must be considered to express the power of multinational corporations. As such, these "cathedrals of commerce" can
reveal important aspects of the economic power that governs our
time. It is for this reason that they interest us. It is not our intention
here to carry out a formal analysis of the skyscraper, nor to trace
the stages of its development. Our aim, rather, is to use the skyscraper as a powerful magnifying glass, through which to observe
the society that builds it and that inhabits the spaces created by it.

The skyscraper's image has great potential as an advertising image,
and because of this its principal goal has become that of attracting
the attention of the public. Only when considered in this light can
the skyscraper's periodic transformations be understood. The basic
aim of an advertising image is to attract attention and to remind the
public of the product it is promoting. To maintain the kind of publicity bombardment to which our society has been subjected for
decades demands an unceasing and almost virtuoso hunt for new
ways to capture the attention of an increasingly indifferent public.
The Post-Modern style, the most recent image of American skyscrapers, is one example of this.

The Post-Modern style has become increasingly unpopular. Even
Philip Johnson, the architect who first used it in skyscraper design,
now privately criticizes and disavows it, while those critics who gave
their support to the Post-Modern style at the beginning of the eight-
ies have now begun to distance themselves from it. This comes as
no surprise. Evidently a new look is being prepared for the skyscraper
of the future—the same was true of the International style of the
late 1970s and also will be true of the fashion worn by skyscrapers
in the next few years. Yet perhaps there is another reason for this

disavowal, one that has more to do with the nature of the Post-Modern style itself than with the mere routine passing of trends. The search for something shocking, for an eye-catching form, has almost reached the point of exhaustion. In their quest for the sensational, American architects, and Philip Johnson first among them, have resorted to using images that are certainly powerful, but whose power is something akin to a slap in the face, a power that is more overpowering than majestic.

This study attempts to stitch back together the skyscraper's "image" and its "content." In our society, the world of images (and therefore of imagination, but also of illusions) has acquired an excessive and worrisome importance. It is as if a mass exodus from content—and therefore from reality—were underway. Images no longer seem to have any referents, but rather to have become ends in themselves. Yet it only *seems* this way; actually, images result from a precise set of motives that will appear to be quite obvious if we take the time to look at them. The Post-Modern style may already have reached the end of the road (to everyone's relief), but as the underlying motives and causes that produced it remain, it follows that these motives will simply and predictably find other ways of manifesting themselves.

Our aim in these pages has been to take the most recent of the skyscraper's images (concentrating on the years between the mid-1970s and the mid-1980s), hold them still for a moment, and scrape away the surface in order to discover what it is that these images do not reveal and often hide. We feel that knowledge is an indispensable instrument of self-defense—nobody likes to be slapped in the face.

THE STUDY OF THE PRESENT

When we study the present—that is, the events taking place around us—we are deprived for the most part of that measure of critical distance that permits true observation. We need this detachment, which allows us to place the object of study under our eyes and place it under the scrutiny of our thought as well. In analyzing something in which we are immersed, we lose the privilege granted by a distant viewpoint, which, while "transforming" the object of our attention into something much smaller, allows us a more wide-ranging over-view. A view of the whole—vital for understanding the contours of a figure—is made possible only by distance. From afar we may enjoy a panoramic view: seen from a hill, a city appears enclosed in its boundaries and the eye can take it all in. But upon entering the city (let us say an unknown city) without a map, it is easy to get lost. All one needs is a map.

My special thanks to the studio of Kohn, Pederson, Fox Associates for allowing me to observe the skyscraper from an extraordinary point of view: from the inside.

Late-Twentieth-Century Skyscrapers

1

The Image

THE SKYSCRAPER'S IMAGE

A comparison of the skyscrapers built in large American cities in
the first years of the twentieth century versus those built in the
1930s, the 1960s, and the 1980s, amply demonstrates the skyscraper's
capacity to change its face in a short span of time. Flanking the Art
Deco forms of skyscrapers dating from the 1930s, we find International style or Modern forms created in the decade 1950–1960, as
well as Post-Modern ones from the 1980s. If we go further back in
time, yet another contrast may be added to this set of images: the
image of the skyscrapers built in 1880–1890. There is a reason for
this continual mutation of the skyscraper's form, one that is quite
independent of considerations of structure and function (which have
both remained fundamentally the same) and that can be understood
only if we consider the economic system to which the skyscraper
belongs.

Kenneth Turney Gibbs of Cornell University has conducted an
interesting study of the use of the image of the business building
from 1870 to 1930.[1] Gibbs interprets the various changes of form
in the skyscraper as responses made by the business world to fluctua-
tions in public opinion. According to Gibbs, the appearance of flamboyant forms corresponds to periods in which public opinion is seen
to be rather critical of the business world. In the same way, simple
and essential forms tend to appear during periods in which a fairly
positive public opinion prevails, so that businesspeople feel no press-
ing need to take action.

The skyscraper's changes of form (image might be a better word,
because the skyscraper remains a building of gigantically tall proportions whose form remains substantially the same) are thus the fruit
of an efficient strategy followed by big business in order to curry
favor with public opinion. The transformations undergone by this

powerful image correspond to a courting of public opinion, achieved by means of the seductive power of the image itself, and above all by one of the most powerful images that can be set before human eyes: the architectural image.

From 1976 onward, the skyscraper has assumed a new image, this time baptized with the term *Post-Modern*. This new, flamboyant image has developed in reaction to the austere, essential image of the modern skyscrapers of the 1950s and 1960s. An analysis of this recent transformation may help us understand some aspects of the business world and American multinationals, a world of which the skyscraper is both product and home.

The new, Post-Modern image is not a purely formal phenomenon but is like the tip of an iceberg. The reasons for this singular style or fashion are embodied in the laws that govern economic power and in the mentality that power has produced.

THE PRESS

The press plays an important role in the analysis of the Post-Modern skyscraper. Numerous articles on the subject have been published by newspapers and magazines, particularly architectural and business magazines.

The press is not only a precious source of news; it is also the means by which the holders of economic power—corporate leaders—address public opinion. Articles by architectural journalists (and it is no accident that they are all substantially alike, whether published by the *New York Times*, the *Chicago Tribune*, or *Progressive Architecture*) reveal America's way of thinking in general, or rather, they reveal the way of thinking that the leaders of multinationals want America (and not only America) to adopt. Articles published in the American press reinforce the image of the Post-Modern skyscraper, following word for word the reasoning of the advertising:

> *Advertising canons work on a double register: a) verbal; b) visual. As has been widely demonstrated, the verbal register's chief function is to anchor the message, since the visual message often appears ambiguous, conceptualizable in various ways.*[2]

Mass Media

In a sense, Post-Modern architecture is closely linked to the logic of mass media. These skyscrapers constitute an architecture directed at men and women who are accustomed to strong visual stimuli. They are addressed to a public that is accustomed to receiving advertising communications and is therefore accustomed to associating advertising images with advertising talk.

The forms of Post-Modern skyscrapers have the precise function of attracting attention. What the public should think of these forms (images) is in turn written in magazines and newspapers. Articles about skyscrapers, therefore, have the same referential value that the verbal register has for advertising images. They are a medium for speaking to the public about architecture. Or, rather, the press is the medium used to let people know what they should think of this architecture. The skyscrapers themselves have only a secondary, symbolic role in all this, since it is clear that what public opinion must be favorable toward is what skyscrapers represent: the world of business.

In this regard, we should take into account the huge importance of public opinion for the corporate system. As E. K. Hall, vice president of AT&T and a pioneer in the development of corporate public relations, has said, unfavorable public opinion represents a serious danger for corporations:

> *Our relationship with the public began with a serious handicap. They didn't know who we were, they misunderstood us, didn't respect us, and there was a constant tendency to believe that we didn't have the right intentions as far as they were concerned . . . Such a general attitude of mind in the public is, I believe, not just a serious danger for the "property of the business" but is, in my opinion, the only serious danger for the corporation, because the natural tendency of such hostility . . . may at any moment lead to its fossilization into some form of adverse legislation.[3]*

Together the press and the skyscraper constitute a powerful means of mass communication, of iconographic persuasion directed at an impressionable public.

The power of mass communication is touched on by Konrad Lorenz, who enumerates eight deadly sins of our society, among them "the indoctrination process." He begins by saying that people now exhibit a greater readiness than ever before to be indoctrinated, and he continues:

> *The increase in numbers of people within a single cultural group, together with the perfection of technical means, lead to the possibility of maneuvering public opinion into a uniformity unprecedented in the history of mankind. Furthermore, the suggestive effect of an accepted doctrine grows with the number of its supporters, possibly in geometric progression. There are cultures in which an individual who purposely keeps aloof from the influence of mass media, for example from television, is regarded as pathological. Deindividualizing effects are desired by all those whose intention it is to manipulate large bodies of people. Opinion polls, advertising, cleverly directed fads and fashions help the mass producers on this side of the iron curtain, and the functionaries on the other side to attain what amounts to a similar power over the masses.[4]*

The Architectural Press

Skidmore, Owings and Merrill's Lever House and Mies van der Rohe's Seagram Building, built in New York in 1952 and 1958, respectively, are considered by American architectural journalists to be the most important representatives of Modern or International Style skyscrapers and therefore directly responsible for the proliferation of "glass boxes" that beset American cities in the 1960s. Indeed, the architectural press goes so far as to identify this phenomenon as one of the principal causes of the ills that afflict American metropolises today.

The Seagram Building and Lever House are accorded a degree of respect and a recognized right to continued existence—a real exception to the process of endless demolition and rebuilding that is part of the reality of most skyscrapers.[5] As forerunners of the International Style, however, they and the architects who designed them are nonetheless held responsible for the "detrimental change" of the American city.

The pioneers (or prototypes) of the Post-Modern skyscraper were certain skyscrapers built during the mid-1970s whose form, unlike the glass box design of the Modern skyscraper, showed such variations as broken-off tops, rounded corners, and widened bases. Examples of this type are the IDS Center in Minneapolis and Pennzoil Place in Houston, designed by Philip Johnson and John Burgee and built in 1972 and 1976, respectively; the Transamerica Building, designed by William Pereira (San Francisco, 1977); and the Citicorp Building, designed by Hugh Stubbins and Associates (New York, 1977).

The first true Post-Modern skyscraper is the AT&T building. The changes that distinguished the first Post-Modern prototypes from the Modern style skyscraper were limited to a series of geometric variations. But in his design for the AT&T, Philip Johnson introduced a new type of variation: the *historical quotation*.

Below is a series of excerpts from various newspaper and magazine articles on the Post-Modern skyscraper. Several common themes run through them, indicating that the architectural press has reached something of a consensus on this style. The most basic theme is the revolt against the "boring glass box."

The prototypes of Post-Modern skyscrapers: **Facing page**—Pennzoil Place, Houston, 1976, Johnson/Burgee Architects (Photo: Richard Payne); **page 6**—The Trans-America Building, San Francisco, 1977, William Pereira Architect (Photo: Dida Biggi); **page 7**—Citicorp Center, New York, 1977, The Stubbins Associates and Emery Roth & Sons, Associate Architects. (Photo: Edward Jacoby)

The design of office buildings finds itself now in a state of transition, not to say ferment. During the 1960s, building developers saw that the esthetic and intellectual rigor imposed on the building type by Mies van der Rohe was susceptible to low-cost knock-offs, and architects grew to despise the derivative, boring "office box." Some, like Michael Graves at Portland, Oregon, have attacked their boredom by applying a new decorative face to the form. Others, like Philip Johnson at Pennzoil in Houston, have attacked it by rethinking the shape of such buildings.

The New York City firm Kohn Pedersen Fox Associates wants to have it both ways, and it is in the process of establishing a convincing claim to success.[6]

If there is any encouraging sign in American architecture right now, it is that certain ideas which seemed somewhat radical just a few years ago— and were the exclusive province of a group of noncommercial, "high design" architects—have begun the great journey into the rest of the culture. I am speaking most particularly of the tendency away from the austerity of orthodox modern architecture and toward an architecture that re-uses historical forms, accepts the possibility of ornament, and emphasizes the relationship of a building to its neighbors.
When the American Telephone & Telegraph Company in 1978 accepted the design of Philip Johnson and John Burgee for a 37-story, granite-sheathed skyscraper in midtown Manhattan with a Renaissance-inspired bottom and a Chippendale-inspired top, that was a significant event— a kind of beginning of this journey, the first instance of the acceptance of what has come to be called "Post-Modern" architecture by a rich and powerful corporation.[7]

After a long run of anonymous corporate architecture, companies are once again using buildings to capture the public's attention. This pattern probably started with Houston's Pennzoil Place—pointed twin towers designed by Philip Johnson that appear to change their shapes as you drive around the city. The slanted top, elegant metal-and-glass skin and lively atrium of New York's Citicorp Center, designed by Hugh Stubbins & Associates, literally gave that giant financial institution a new corporate profile. Several other Johnson buildings, such as his glass Gothic tower for PPG in Pittsburgh and the "Chippendale" AT&T headquarters under construction in New York, are more shocking in their appearance than anything by Kohn Pedersen Fox. But no firm is more successful than Kohn Pedersen Fox in popularizing design innovations while working for conventional companies and developers.[8]

For the last 30 years, the crisp, austere forms of the International Style have been the hallmark of this city's skyline. So one's first reaction to the latest crop of Chicago skyscrapers is that they don't belong here—that there has been some mistake, that they must have been intended for some other city.
But that is not, of course, the case—the half-dozen or so new buildings that are so completely changing this city's skyline were very much meant to be here, and what they proved is that Chicago, like the rest of the country, has moved away from the rigid orthodoxies of the International Style. The change from blank boxes to more eccentric skyscraper forms has been slower to come to this city than to most others, but it has now arrived in earnest.[9]

The American Telephone & Telegraph corporate headquarters, New York, 1985, Johnson/Burgee Architects. (Photo: Richard Payne)

For the better part of the last twenty years, everyone has been complaining about those "boring office buildings". But until recently no one has done much about it. The main reason those "cereal boxes" have popped up like dandelions is that (to quote from this month's article on new tower designs) "developers saw that the esthetic and intellectual rigor imposed on the building type by Mies van der Rohe was susceptible to low-cost knock-offs." That was just what most client/developers wanted, and their architects went ahead and designed them until the "better streets" of many of our cities are literally lined with these corporate clones. And most of those new buildings have generated about as much excitement and enthusiasm as a new dandelion.

There was a time when the arrival of a "new" skyscraper was a real event. Raymond Hood's Chicago Tribune Tower and Cass Gilbert's Woolworth Building and William Van Alen's Chrysler Building (and a host of others like them) made an impact on their cities, made an impact on the public, and made an impact on architectural thought. They were exciting!

Well, the excitement is coming back. Across the country we see rising a whole new breed of "skyscrapers"—buildings that make a mark on the skyline, that have individuality, that relate to the public passing by or through. Buildings that relate not just to the bottom line, but to the new concerns imposed by energy costs, and the new concerns about fitting their urban context.

PPG Place: detail of view at street
level, Pittsburgh, 1983, Johnson/Burgee
Architects. (Photo: Richard Payne)

*When did the new excitement start? You can pick your own "first
glimmer"—and somebody will surely write a book on "The Origins of
the New Skyscraper" about five years from now. For me (though it was
mostly a technological experiment) SOM's 'Big John' Hancock in Chicago
(Record, January 1967) seems an important pioneer for its height, its
shape, and its mixed-use. More recently, and more vividly, Johnson
Burgee's Pennzoil Place in Houston (November 1967) got clients and architects
alike thinking—not just because it was strikingly handsome and exuberant
building, and not just because it was designed by a firm whose work al-
ways attracts study, but because it was commissioned by Gerald Hines—
who is surely one of the most thoughtful, cost-conscious, and successful
developers ever. And then there is Hugh Stubbins' Citicorp (Record,*

*1978)—which surely makes a mark on the skyline with its slanted top
and shiny skin. . . . And lately, we've been seeing more and more new
towers that deserve careful study. In March, we published five new office
buildings by SOM, and not one of them is anything like a "boring box."* [10]

*While [Pennzoil Place] revolutionized Modernist glass boxes, [Republic-
Bank Center] symbolizes not only the architect's boredom with those boxes,
but reveals, as does the AT&T, their desire to put the romance back into
skyscrapers. Romantic is hardly the word. Behind a twelve-story banking
hall with a stepped, gabled roof and a monumental entrance arch rises
a tower that steps up twice to create the illusion of three towers . . . In
fact, the bank wanted . . . a more "traditional" design that would distinguish it from its Modern neighbours . . . Like Pennzoil, Republic Bank
uses stepbacks and angles to create its own identity . . . But from any distance at all, the building's Expressionist power is captivating. It can appear
alternately fanciful, energetic, and brooding . . ."* [11]

The Verbal Register

The biggest obstacle to our understanding of what the press has
to say about the Post-Modern skyscraper is the journalists' and critics'
choice of terms. That Johnson's design for the Republic Bank should
be defined as "traditional," for instance, is somewhat perplexing, and
it is no less surprising to read that the base of the AT&T Building
is Renaissance-inspired. The statement that "historical forms" are being reemployed is very vague, and what exactly is meant by "modern"
architecture, anyway? To which architects does the term refer, which
nations, which buildings? The language adopted by the press is repetitive and evasive, and only *appears* to be simple and clear—the very
language, in fact, that is commonly used in the advertising and business worlds. And while such language is capable of producing excellent results when used in its proper place, when transposed to the architectural field it becomes obscure and difficult to understand. It
is a language that lends itself to repetition rather than comprehension.

The slogan is a phrase clothed in an easily remembered form.
It is therefore brief, simple, and rhythmic. A slogan is above all
something to be repeated, and not by one person but by groups of
people. It serves to excite, to create enthusiasm, to engender a feeling
of cohesion and participation. It must be contagious and exhilarating.
It does not necessarily have to be logical, nor does it have to be gram-
matically correct. Its purpose is to communicate not mere concepts
but emotions, sensations.

Slogans are not meant to be analyzed or understood, since they
aim only to create favorable feelings and emotions toward whatever
they promote. In the case of the architectural press, their use of

Right—Northwestern Terminal, Chicago, 1985, Murphy/Jahn Architects. (Photo: Murphy/Jahn Architects)

Facing page—The Republic Bank Center towering over Pennzoil Place, Houston, 1984, Johnson/Burgee Architects. (Photo: Richard Payne)

slogan-like repetitive phasing serves to create a consensus of opinion
concerning both skyscrapers and the enormous business activity
that their construction entails and houses.

The Architectural Journalists' View

Most architectural journalists hailed the advent of the Post-Modern
style as the end of a long period of boredom and the beginning of
a new era in American architecture. However, their articles on the
subject rarely come to grips with the reasons why this change should
have come about. Even Paul Goldberger, architectural journalist
for the *New York Times*, in his book on skyscrapers confines himself

The American Telephone & Telegraph's
Romanesque tower base, New York,
1985, Johnson/Burgee Architects.
(Photo: Richard Payne)

to declaring that the demise of the International style—the "corporate
style" of the period 1950–1970—was due to its ultimate failure to
respond to the needs of its clients. Goldberger claims that the reason
for the skyscrapers' change of form was economic—not only
aesthetic—but he does not elaborate on this statement.[12]

As we have seen, architectural journalists tend to limit themselves
to declaring that at long last, architects have stopped building boring
glass boxes and have taken to designing skyscrapers that are varied
and pleasing and that also have such merits as taking account of the
context into which they are to be inserted, making use of decorations
and colors, reaffirming historical links by reemploying architectural
forms from the past, and possessing a precise identity that is in turn
conferred upon the city in which the skyscraper is built.

The Business World's View

The business world's view is that a successful building image must be a powerful advertising instrument. And a successful building image is first and foremost an image that captures the public's attention. The Post-Modern style satisfies these requirements, while the International style no longer does.

Just what kind of response an "eye-catching" form can elicit in the public was clearly demonstrated in 1976 by the building of Pennzoil Place, a skyscraper whose form was a modification of the Modern style skyscraper. In fact, Pennzoil's dazzling form succeeded in increasing the real estate value of the skyscraper and in creating an image of success for the Pennzoil Corporation, which registered a significant increase in applications for employment after the skyscraper's construction. But the effects produced by Pennzoil Place were not so much dependent on its form *per se* as on the fact that its neighboring skyscrapers were of the simple parallelepipedal type. In fact, an eye-catching form is a form that contrasts strongly with its surroundings. This is a very important point in the history of the skyscraper's changes of image and one to which we shall return.

The pyramidal skyscraper designed by William Pereira and built in 1977 in San Francisco confirms the same fact: its success was due to the singularity of its form (and not its beauty, its functionality, or other factors). Further confirmation of positive effects produced (on business) by the modern skyscraper's change of image is provided by the Citicorp Center, designed by Hugh Stubbins and Associates, also in 1977. The enormous oblique top of Citicorp, which stands out as an eminently recognizable feature of the Manhattan skyline, has not only resulted in an increase of the building's real estate value but has also created a winning image for its client, Citibank. In almost every single advertisement for this important financial institution (not only in newspapers but in leaflets distributed to thousands of the bank's branches throughout America), Stubbins's skyscraper appears as the company's hallmark.

Outlays for good design are also like expenditures for corporate image advertising. Says Houston developer Gerald D. Hines, president of Gerald D. Hines Interests: "Companies spend a lot of money in advertising their image. They can cut that back if they have an outstanding building that gains national attention." A successful building image can also translate into more rental dollars. "Good architecture really helped New York's Citicorp Center," says one observer. "It has a skin that caught everybody's imagination, shape at the top, and large public areas . . . [which include a skylit atrium draped with plantings and lined with shops and restaurants]. It's not in a great location, but it gets one of the highest rents in Manhattan," he says.[13]

The financial benefits are substantial as well:

Able to rent the building at a premium that real estate people estimate at 20 percent or more, Citibank Chairman Walter B. Wriston never moved himself or the majority of bank offices into the new structure. The design of Houston's Pennzoil Place also paid off in rents that command a premium of three to four dollars per square foot, says developer Hines. And the building also helped Pennzoil Co. to attract geologists and engineers. "In a competitive job market," Hines says, "people want to work for a company that represents more than just a commodity in space." [14]

The shift in styles was inexorable:

At the same time that owners became more interested in architecture, a variety of fresh and individualized styles in architecture began making their debut. More and more, these new styles got the nod over the neat, minimally designed glass-and-metal rectangular towers inspired by the International style, a popular form of office architecture from the 1950s to the 1970s. [15]

The Architectural and Business Press

Business magazines openly declare that the Post-Modern image of the skyscraper has had a very positive effect on profits (of developers, corporate managers, architects, and all of the businesses involved in the construction industry). Curiously, architectural journalists are not so explicit on this subject. The activities of business people and those of architects are seen by the latter as belonging to two separate worlds, when in reality, and above all in the case of the skyscraper, the two go hand in hand. As early as 1920, William Corbett defined the skyscraper as "a machine for making money." [16]

Discussions of the Post-Modern skyscraper published in architectural magazines show a tendency to gloss over such matters. They concentrate on the skyscraper's image, its relationship with its context and with the past, its presumed human scale, its invigorating qualities. No mention is made of the real-world factors of which the skyscraper is a product, nor of the sort of requirements that its image must meet. The veiled message that comes across is that skyscrapers exist for the good of people—which is just what business wants people to think—while the truth is that they exist for the good of business. And despite the fact that there is a tendency in America to identify the one with the other, they are not the same thing. (In this context, the popular success of a book such as Thomas J. Peters and Robert H. Waterman Jr.'s *In Search of Excellence*, published in 1982, is significant. After analyzing the behavior of the most important corporations, the authors recommend that in order to achieve a similar kind of excellence, similar behavior patterns should be followed by individuals—as if every single man or woman, in order to be successful in life, should act like a multinational.) [17]

Facing page—Citicorp Center, as depicted in a 1989 advertisement for Citibank. (Courtesy Citibank, N.A.)

CITICORP CELEBRATES AMERICA.

CITICORP AND CITIBANK PRESENT THE WORLD'S LARGEST ILLUMINATED AMERICAN FLAGS AND A LASER LIGHT SHOW ON JULY 3RD AND 4TH.

Citicorp and Citibank cordially invite you to see the third annual unfurling of the world's largest illuminated Star Spangled Banner at 9:00 pm on Monday, July 3rd, and Tuesday, July 4th.

It's a celebration of America highlighted by a spectacular laser light show synchronized to music broadcast over WNSR 105.1 FM. Tune in WNSR each night at 9 pm to hear fifteen minutes of patriotic rock 'n' roll to accompany a dazzling laser display on the east and west sides of Citicorp Center. The flags and lasers will be visible for miles until 2 am, from anywhere the upper floors of Citicorp Center at 53rd and Lexington can be seen.

Take a few minutes this long weekend to celebrate America with our Star Spangled Spectacular. It's our way of expressing pride in all that makes this country great. Happy 213th Birthday, America.

CITICORP◆CITIBANK®

WNSR
105FM

© Copyright Citicorp/Citibank 1989

FOR MORE INFORMATION, CALL 1-800-722-7276

17

MODERN/POST-MODERN

The most prominent American architectural firms design Post-Modern skyscrapers. Naturally, the designs differ from one firm to the next: Helmut Jahn's skyscraper designs are different from those of Skidmore, Owings and Merrill, just as Philip Johnson's vary from those of Kohn Pedersen Fox Associates. But they all have one important thing in common: a strong reaction against designs of the Modern or International style type.

The characteristics of the Post-Modern skyscraper seem to have evolved as a kind of antidote to what American architectural journalists see as the characteristics of the Modern skyscraper. The Modern skyscraper, with its parallelepipedal form, appeared as an isolated object in the city, while the Post-Modern skyscraper (so it is said) becomes an integral part of its context. Modern design produced skyscrapers that are the result of a rarefaction of the form, of the destruction of formal values; Post-Modern design produces skyscrapers that are varied, colored, decorated. There is hardly anything to distinguish one Modern style skyscraper from the next; the Post-Modern skyscraper is distinctive, original. It possesses, it is said, an identity. In the Modern skyscraper those parts dedicated to aesthetic perception (the base and the top) have been eliminated, and the facade consists of a succession of identical floors; in the Post-Modern skyscraper, the whole is dedicated to aesthetic perception. In its transformation of skyscrapers into simple glass parallelepipeds, Modern design took meaning away from architectural language; Post-Modern design, it is said, gives architectural language a new meaning.

A New Language

The architects of Post-Modern skyscrapers are said to have created a new architectural language. What, we may ask, after the nullification of architectural forms carried out in Lever House and Seagram, and above all in the thousands of copies that they inspired, has been the source of these new "words"?

For one, architects have taken inspiration from the forms of skyscrapers built before the glass box period; another source has been the architecture that preceded modern architecture. (*Modern architecture* appears here as something very vague, a kind of mist out of which only the International style skyscraper seems to emerge with any clarity.) The answer, then, is more or less everything: from Ancient Greek to Gothic, from Renaissance to Art Deco. The new architectural language thus originates from all architectural forms of the past, deformed and introduced into the new context of present-day America.

Facing page—Post-Modern skyscrapers: PPG Place, Pittsburgh, 1983, Johnson/Burgee Architects. (Photo: Richard Payne)

Above—Rendering of PPG Place, Pittsburgh, 1983, Johnson/Burgee Architects.

Facing page—Riverside view of PPG Place, Pittsburgh, 1983, Johnson/Burgee Architects. (Photo: Richard Payne)

Identity and Symbol

The term "identity" recurs frequently in discussions of Post-Modern skyscrapers and this demonstrates, if nothing else, the uniformity of linguistic usage. However, this insistence that architecture must confer "identity" leads us to suspect a disturbing lack of it, on both the individual and the group levels. In fact, the diversity and peculiarity of Post-Modern forms make them very distinct from the parallelepipedal forms of the Modern style skyscraper. The issue of identity is thus confused with distinctiveness, with recognizability, with standing out from the rest. And all these terms, it should be noted, have to do with external, superficial appearances, while for human beings identity is a problem with much deeper roots.

There is also much talk of symbols. The forms to which symbolic value is here attributed are, in reality, visual messages whose aim is to attract attention, to strike the imagination and impress themselves on the memory. They are not forms capable of provoking a profound response in the observer. In the words of Rudolph Arnheim:

> *An image serves merely as a* sign *to the extent to which it stands for a particular content without reflecting its characteristics visually . . . the characteristics signs tend to be selected in such a way as to serve their function. In this sense, they are not arbitrary. Discussing visual "effectors," Konrad Lorenz has observed that the simplicity of shape and color makes them distinct in appearance and "improbable" in occurrence, that is unlikely to be confused with other things visible in the environment. To the extent to which images are signs, they can serve only as indirect media, for they operate as mere references to the things for which they stand. They are not analogues, and therefore they cannot be used as media for thought in their own right.[18]*

It is difficult to believe that these terms—identity and symbol—are used by mistake; on the contrary, a precise motive lies behind their use. To state that Post-Modern skyscrapers confer identity on a city and its inhabitants is to accord them some form of social commitment. In fact, eulogies of these skyscrapers are often followed by an attack on Modern skyscrapers, which are supposedly guilty, because of their glass box form, of having rendered cities indistinguishable from one another and having thus deprived them of their identity.

In the same way, to consider the forms of these skyscrapers as images with symbolic value implies a desire to attribute some great communicative capacity to this architecture. If the form of one corporation's skyscraper is distinguishable from that of others, this is taken to signify that the corporation stands out against its competitors; if the skyscraper is faced with granite or limestone rather than with glass, it means that that corporation is strong and solid; if the skyscraper is situated in the city center, it means that the corporation occupies a key position in the life of the society; if the form of the skyscraper in some way echoes the forms of the architecture of the past, it means that the corporation has strong traditions; and so on.

A useful tool in our analysis of the forms of these skyscrapers is provided by Arnheim's examination of the distinguishing marks of the Chase Manhattan Bank:

> *A good modern trademark interprets the character of its bearer by associating it with clearly defined patterns of visual forces. An example of this is the famous emblem of the Chase Manhattan Bank designed by Chermayeff and Geismar. The square interior and octagonal exterior produce a centrally balanced form which conveys a sense of repose, unity, solidity.*

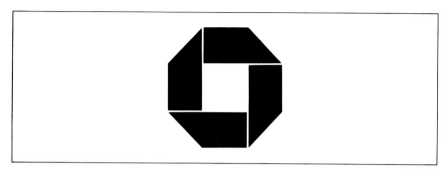

The Chase Manhattan Bank, North America, symbol. (Design: Chermayeff & Geismar Associates)

Like a fortress, it is closed off against any interference, and is unaffected by the changes and the vicissitudes of the times, while possessing the necessary vitality and sense of purpose to carry out a function. The sharp edges of its components introduce dynamic forces which do not, however, undermine the form as a whole, but remain confined within the fixed structure, without directional pull. The rival motions balance each other out in a lively general hush, or they combine to produce the continuous, controlled rotation of an engine . . .[19]

Whereas a classical building may be likened to a language and broken down into words (arches, architraves, columns, capitals, and so on) or phrases (made up of combinations of the preceding elements), the skyscraper may be compared to a hieroglyphic structure, which only can be broken down into subelements at the risk of losing all communicative capacity. In this sense, skyscrapers can be taken as either a regression to an archaic architectonic script, or a first attempt at a new language (architectonic or urban?).

The Deformation of Familiar Forms to Attract Attention

Let us consider some phrases from Paul Goldberger's book, *The Skyscraper.* In the following passage he looks at the great pioneer of Post-Modern skyscrapers: Pennzoil Place, designed by Philip Johnson.

. . . Pennzoil Place, in Houston, completed in 1976, became the best-known building in that booming city's downtown with good reason: it was a pair of trapezoid-shaped towers, each sliced off at a 45-degree angle at the top, and joined at the bottom by a communal greenhouse lobby. This was pure abstraction, but it was dazzling—a city had not seen so recognizable a skyscraper top since the Empire State Building's. And the twin trapezoids, for all their energy, had a certain dignity, too—it was Johnson's gift that he was able to create an eye-catching form just right for the image of this city, a place eager to make its mark yet desirous of appearing strong and stable at the same time.[20]

If we look carefully at the adjectives used by Goldberger to describe Pennzoil Place's form ("dazzling," "recognizable," "eye-catching"), we will understand what basic features constitute a successful form for the skyscraper.

We should also note that the skyscraper is interpreted here in terms of the sensations or emotions that it produces in the spectator. This is quite natural, since the form of these skyscrapers aims precisely to provoke emotions such as surprise, wonder, exaltation.

One fundamental characteristic must be borne in mind when speaking of skyscrapers: height. Just to see a skyscraper grow into a giant in the space of a few years is something shocking. The amount of work involved in planning and building a skyscraper is enormous, especially if one considers the short time into which all this work is compressed. As few as three years may pass from the start of planning to the completion of construction work. The sight of skyscrapers continually being built, demolished, and rebuilt is, to say the least, astonishing. The actual effort involved in this almost endless process is tangible, and the sight of skyscrapers taking on such forms only adds to the sense of wonder.

Goldberger speaks of a tendency in contemporary American architecture that leads architects to "reemploy historical forms," to reconsider decorative effects, and to reestablish a "relationship with the context." In discussing buildings such as the AT&T, however, the *Times* critic gives no explanation of the real substance of Philip Johnson's brilliant intuition; that is, uprooting an element from its original context (it is hard to say whether this element is architectonic or decorative: how to define the vague yet precise resemblance between the AT&T top and the decorative motifs used to crown certain pieces of early nineteenth-century English furniture?), deforming it by means of a simple enlargement of scale, and placing it in a wholly new context. This is because in his discussions of architecture, Goldberger does not take into consideration the motives that guide it and the ends for which a building is built. And this ignores the fact that a skyscraper has a cast-iron economic motive. Philip Johnson—as he revealed to Goldberger in an interview, parts of which were published by the *Times* in September 1977 (i.e., a year after the completion of Pennzoil)—had been searching "for ways to make aesthetic statements economically viable."[21] In other words, he was working on skyscraper images that would attract the commercial attention of the public. Pennzoil was shocking because it stood out from Modern style skyscrapers; AT&T achieves the same effect, but for more complex reasons. Its top is the product of a deformation of a universally recognized decorative motif. The deformation of familiar images produces an effect of estrangement and is consequently shocking.

Johnson has shown an understanding of the psychology of the masses that is equal to that of his business clients. However, Johnson was only the initiator: there are now numerous architectural firms

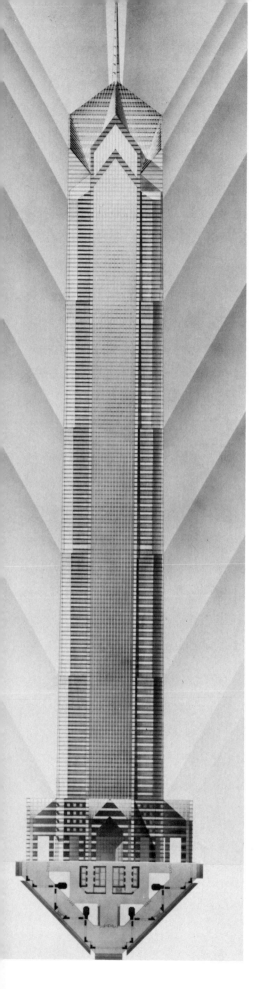

using (deforming) the forms of past architectures in their skyscraper designs.

Past architectural forms clearly inspired the work of William Pedersen, design partner in the firm of Kohn Pedersen Fox Associates, in his designs for the Proctor and Gamble headquarters and in the commercial skyscrapers recently built in New York, Chicago, and Pittsburgh. Helmut Jahn, in his enlargement of the Chicago Board of Trade premises, executed a kind of duplication of the existing building and in general draws inspiration from Art Deco skyscrapers. Another example of this trend is provided by the firm of Hardy, Holzman, Pfeiffer Associates, whose designs for Best Products headquarters are a veritable collage of elements taken from widely diverse architectonic-decorative sources. We could go on citing examples until we had included almost every single American architectural firm.

In 1982, Century Development Corporation and Southwest Bancshares International of Houston announced an architectural competition for Southwest Bank's general headquarters. Regarding the skyscraper's desired image, the competition advertisement stated:

> The tower shall project an INSTITUTIONAL, TIMELESS character. It should have a prominent architectural profile on the Houston skyline. The architectural form should be distinctive and become a SYMBOL of the project and its CENTRAL presence in downtown Houston. The form of the base should express the strength and substantial nature of a major BANKING INSTITUTION and make a major ENTRY STATEMENT. Inherent in the Bank's concept of institutionality and strength are certain biases for THREE-DIMENSIONAL or MODULATED EXTERIOR wall surfaces and against "GLASS WALL ARCHITECTURE." The Bank's identity should be established more through the building's importance as an overall architectural statement than through its public banking facilities within the building.

Helmut Jahn's winning entry shows, if one reads between the lines, that what was actually requested was a form that dazzles. (Note the customary assault on International style skyscrapers—"glass wall architecture.")

VARIETY AND EXCITEMENT

During the 1930s, Elton Mayo, a Harvard professor engaged in management organization research, conducted a series of experiments. The most famous of these experiments resulted in what is known as

The Bank of Southwest competition: elevation, first entry, Houston, 1982, Murphy/Jahn Architects. (Courtesy Murphy/Jahn Architects)

the "Hawthorne effect." Using workshops at the Hawthorne Works of the Western Electric plant at Cicero, Illinois, Professor Mayo attempted to demonstrate that an improvement of working conditions could increase the workers' level of productivity. To this end, he increased the intensity of the lighting and obtained an increase in productivity. Some time later, he reduced light levels back to their former intensity and, surprisingly, productivity increased yet again. The positive effects on productivity were caused not so much by the intensity of illumination as by the fact that it was varied.[22]

It would seem that the same principle applies to the periodic change of form in the skyscraper. We may now add something to Kenneth Gibbs's thesis, referred to at the beginning of the chapter, and observe that as far as the Post-Modern skyscraper is concerned, it seems that it is not so much its flamboyant image that incites favorable public opinion (which Gibbs considers to be the principal goal of the business building's image), as the fact that it differs from the skyscrapers that preceded it. In other words, it is the variation of the skyscraper's form that attracts public attention—a transitory phenomenon if ever there was one.

The continual mutation of the skyscraper's form is akin to the continual burning of a very powerful collective stimulator. As soon as there is a drop in luminosity, more fuel is thrown on.

THE DESIGN METHOD

The Collage Approach

The facade of 125 East 57th Street, designed by Kohn Pedersen Fox Associates in 1983 for Madison Equities Inc. and built in the heart of Manhattan, is the result of a collage of images. Some are taken from Paul Letarouilly's *Edifices de la Rome moderne*.[23] Others are derived from Art Deco skyscrapers built in New York in the 1920s and 1930s. Looking at the finished product, this is not immediately apparent, since the sources have undergone a massive transformation in their adaptation to new requirements; but if we take the time to examine the design methods followed by the architects, it immediately becomes clearer.

One of this building's two tops recalls the form of a temple (an example perhaps of one of those "nostalgia-producing instruments" identified by Colin Rowe in his book *Collage City*, here catapulted into the New York skyline).[24] The way the windows are grouped both vertically and horizontally, the use of limestone facing, and the effect created by spandrels placed beneath or at the side of the windows are all elements that owe their inspiration to Art Deco skyscrapers built in New York in the 1920s and 1930s. The decorative solution for corner windows repeats Van Alen's design for the

Paper model of 125 East 57th Street, New York, 1988, Kohn Pedersen Fox Associates. (Photo: Jock Pottle)

Chrysler Building; the small, oval piazza in front of the main entrance recalls the elliptical form of the Villa Pia courtyard and the geometric pavement design of the loggia of the Palazzo di Firenze; the skyscraper's base is the result of a reworking of the facade of the *casino* at Villa di Papa Giulio; the column-pilaster-column motif in the colonnade surrounding the corner piazza is taken from the portico of Palazzo dei Conservatori in Rome's Piazza del Campidoglio.[25]

The forms of architecture of the past are adopted much as "objets trouvés, stimulants, a-temporal and necessarily transcultural," as Colin Rowe writes in *Collage City*.[26] In his description of the method followed in designing facades for skyscrapers, William Pedersen recalls the words of Colin Rowe:

> *It is suggested that a collage approach, an approach in which objects are conscripted or seduced from out of their context, is—at the present day—the only way of dealing with the ultimate problems of, either or both, utopia and tradition; and the provenance of the architectural objects introduced into the social collage need not be of great consequence. It relates to taste and conviction. The objects can be aristocratic or they can be "folkish," academic or popular. Whether they originate in Pergamum or Dahomey, in Detroit or Dubrovnik, whether their implications are of the twentieth or the fifteenth century, is no great matter.[27]*

Kohn Pedersen Fox's planning method is similar to that followed by many of America's biggest architectural firms.

The study of the works of great architects of the past takes place at the time of planning. Neither the history nor the significance of these works is taken into account, only their design. The form of a castle or a cathedral might be used to sheathe the entire surface of a skyscraper (PPG), a decorative detail might be used to create its top or its base (AT&T). There might be a true jumble of styles, as for instance in the facade of 125 East 57th Street, which incorporates an antique temple, a Michelangelesque colonnade, the facade of a sixteenth-century villa, and certain details from the Chrysler Building. Elsewhere, Venetian street lights, the walls of the Ducal Palace in Venice, and Renaissance fountains are combined—to create the headquarters of Best Products. "Yet," as Umberto Eco remarks:

> *a certain perplexity and sadness remains when we are confronted with immense forms which for us have lost their original suggestive power, and appear instead (given that we attribute them with much less powerful meanings) as messages which are too enormous or too complex for the information they convey to us.[28]*

53rd Street at Third Avenue, New York, 1986, John Burgee Architects with Philip Johnson. (Photo: Dida Biggi)

History

Architectural journalists hold that Post-Modern skyscrapers make use of historical forms. But does being inspired by Romanesque architecture when designing a skyscraper's lobby (AT&T) mean executing wall reliefs that vaguely reproduce the arches of Romanesque buildings? Does history have any part in this?

It may be that such unscrupulous use of architectural works, past and present, has a positive effect on the planning methods followed by architects, freeing them from inhibition, exciting their imagination, and so on; but it cannot be said that the result is to establish a relationship with history, for the simple reason that history is not given the slightest consideration. If by history we understand a succession of events that happened in certain places, at certain times, in certain contexts, then the use of historical references on the part of architects planning Post-Modern skyscrapers is actually *ahistoric*. To respect history means above all to consider that human beings and their works are inseparably bound to the context in which they live

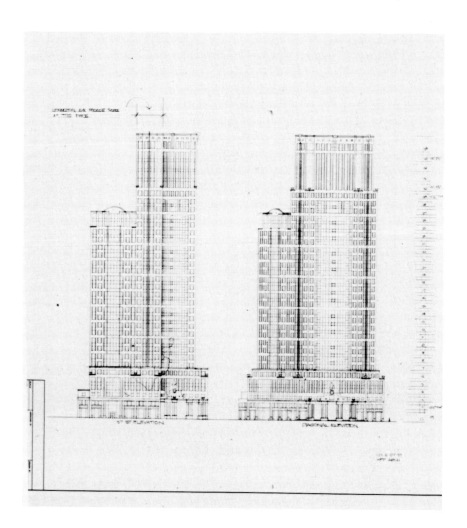

125 East 57th Street: elevation, New York, 1988, Kohn Pedersen Fox Associates. (Photo: Jock Pottle)

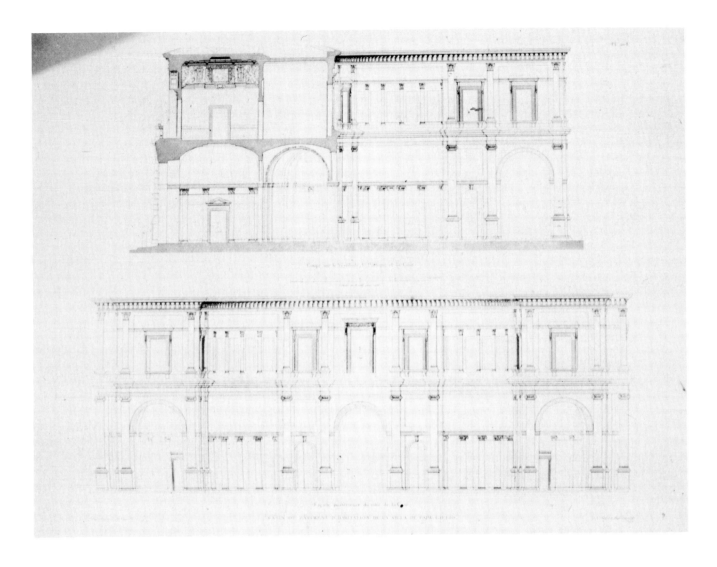

and are produced. What architects and journalists support in words is contradicted in fact. This fluid intermingling of past and present architectural forms makes us suspect some sort of deformation in the perception (and thus the conception) of time.

Planning references, elevation: The Casino at Villa Pia, Rome. (Photo: Jock Pottle)

Time

The only place where time may be frozen into an eternal present is in the imagination. Although the past and the future have continuous links with the present, it is nonetheless important for us to locate them in time, to perceive their distance from the present. In *What's Time Is This Place?* Kevin Lynch writes that a proper perception of time is essential to human health and that the external environment is a major factor in this process. Besides being the products of a distorted perception and conception of time, Post-Modern skyscrapers may also contribute to encouraging such distortion.[29]

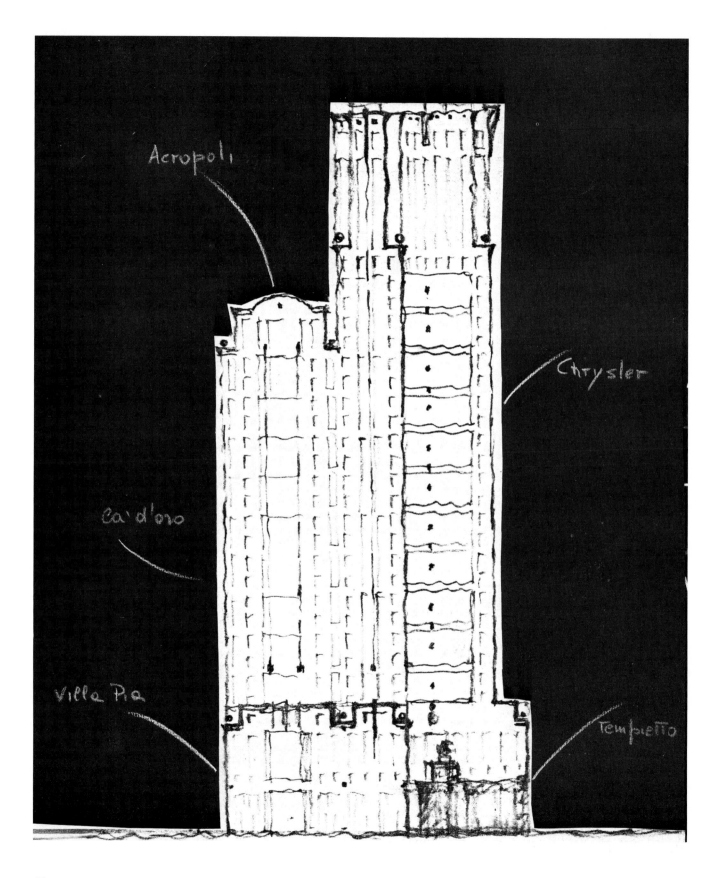

Above—The colonnade of the Palazzo dei Conservatori in the Piazza del Campdoglio, Rome. (Photo: Jock Pottle)

Left—Sketch of 125 East 57th Street, indicating comparative heights of other buildings, New York, 1988, Kohn Pedersen Fox Associates. (Photo: Jock Pottle)

The continual mutation of the skyscraper's image reveals a static vision of architecture in which the time dimension has been suppressed. To concentrate attention solely on the image of buildings and of architectural works suggests that time is lived as a succession of separate moments that make up a whole, and that space is perceived as a series of snapshots. This shattering of time into isolated fragments, in which each moment is immobilized, transfixed, results in the loss of any sense of movement. In order to arrive at a static vision of architecture—an exclusively visual perception in which architecture is transformed into an image—a sort of internal immobility is required. To perceive only the image of space means to suppress its profundity, both metaphorically and literally.

Life is transformed by this fractionized perception of time into a confused mass of frozen instants. Such a vision may make us feel eternal, but this is a neurotic illusion.

Context

Architectural journalists hold that Post-Modern skyscrapers fit well into the context in which they are built. This is a strange affirmation, since if anything characterizes a building such as the AT&T, it is surely the fact that it stands out as quite distinct from the skyscrapers that surround it (or at least it did at the time of its construction: skyscrapers grow quickly). There is more attention paid to the design of the skyscraper's base, that is, to the part directly aimed at the passer-by, but fitting into a context has a more complex meaning than this.

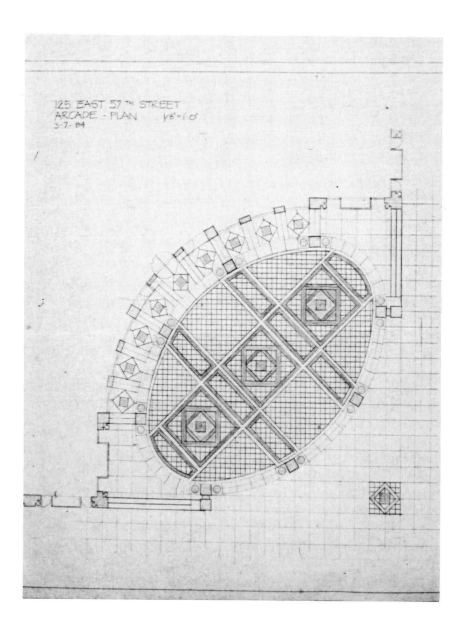

Sketch of the plaza in front of 125 East 57th Street, New York, 1988, Kohn Pedersen Fox Associates. (Photo: Jock Pottle)

229. PLANS OF VILLA PIA IN THE PONTIFICAL GARDEN.
PLAN GÉNÉRAL DE LA VILLA SITUÉE DANS LE JARDIN PONTIFICAL.

Floor plan of the oval piazza of the
Casino at Villa Pia. (Photo: Jock Pottle)

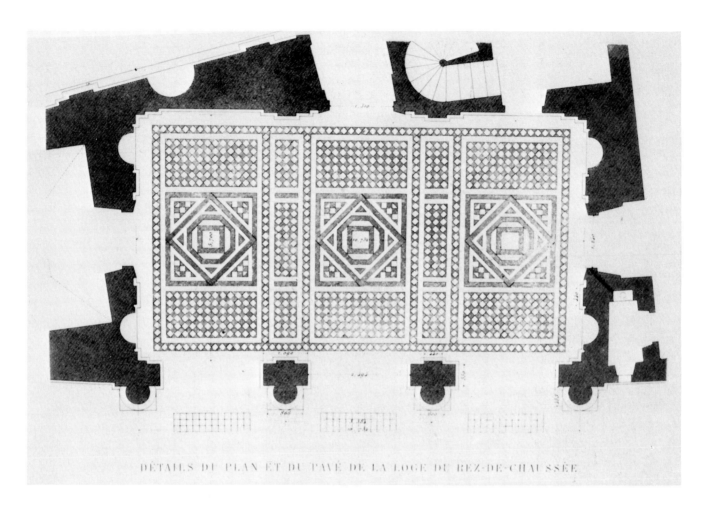

DÉTAILS DU PLAN ET DU PAVÉ DE LA LOGE DU REZ-DE-CHAUSSÉE

Floor plan of plaza in front of 125
East 57th Street, New York, 1988,
Kohn Pedersen Fox Associates. (Photo:
Jock Pottle)

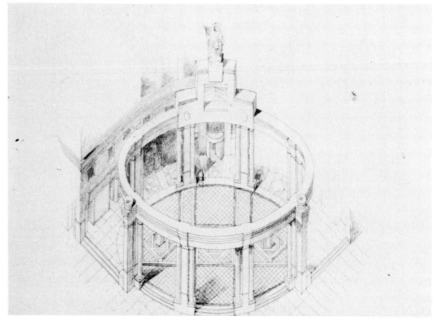

Drawing of the plaza in front of 125
East 57th Street, New York, 1988,
Kohn Pedersen Fox Associates. (Photo:
Jock Pottle)

The oval piazza of the Casino at Villa Pia. (Photo: Jock Pottle)

Post-Modern skyscrapers do not fit into their context (context being understood here in the formal sense of volume, height, decorative detail, etc., and not in the economic, social, political, or historical sense) for the simple reason that their very aim is to be distinct, to stand out from the crowd. In what way do buildings like the AT&T, the PPG, the One South Wacker or the Hercules Building fit into the context for which they were designed? True, they may boast a facing of the same material as was used on the building opposite or next door; they may echo the colors, the forms, or the decorative details of some of the buildings in the vicinity; but they do so in a way that is so distorted and so different that the reference is practically unrecognizable. When confronted by the finished design or the completed building, we have the feeling that we have never before seen anything like it in the world. Yet contextualism is one of the axioms of the Post-Modern style.

Spec Towers Take on a New Look

Developers appear to be abandoning the minimal look, and are jumping on the Post-Modern bandwagon. But the desire to be distinctive does not guarantee distinguished design.

1. Stevenson Place, San Francisco, Calif., Tishman West; Kaplan/McLaughlin/Diaz, architects. 2. Kansas City Place, Kansas City, Mo., Executive Hills Inc.; PBNA architects. 3. Bay Colony, Philadelphia, Pa., Bay Colony; Ballinger Architects. 4. Office tower, Atlanta, Ga., Albritton Development; Chapman Coyle Chapman, architects. 5. AT&T office tower, Kansas City, Mo., AT&T; Howard Needles Tammen & Bergendoff, architects. 6. Office tower, Pittsburgh, Pa., Jenkins Empire Associates; Stubbins Associates, architects. 7. Momentum Place, Dallas, Texas, Cadillac Fairview, MBank; John Burgee with Philip Johnson, architects. 8. City tower, Orange, Calif., Tishman West, Metropolitan Life; Daniel Dworsky, architect.

Eight Post-Modern towers. (Courtesy *Progressive Architecture*, Penton Publishing, July 1985, p. 78)

The Human Scale

Despite the fact that Post-Modern skyscrapers are both bigger and taller than their International style predecessors, it is said that they respect the human scale, whereas the latter did not. In support of this statement, it is pointed out that the Post-Modern introduction of setbacks and variations on the basic parallelepipedal form creates a visual interruption of the skyscraper's height and thus reduces it.[30] The particular attention paid to the design of the skyscraper's base is said to produce the same effect. Yet paying greater attention to the skyscraper's base cannot modify the space that the skyscraper creates. It is impossible to design a city on a human scale simply by concentrating attention on the base or on some other surface feature of structures that, by their very nature, contribute to the creation of cities that are completely out of scale, as if people, walking or driving around the city, were unaware of the gigantic scale of skyscrapers and stopped seeing or sensing them after the fourth or fifth floor. The skyscraper, whether International style, Post-Modern, Art Deco, or whatever other name one cares to use, is by definition a structure not on a human scale.

But the assertion that Post-Modern skyscrapers are on a human scale is a meaningful one nevertheless. If we hold it up to the light, we see only too clearly that it forms part of a continued attempt on the level of surface, illusion, and image to make up for a deficiency in reality.

This talk of context, history, and human scale evidently does not refer to reality. It is rather a message ("Post-Modern is good") that the corporate world wishes to transmit; but the terms used (Post-Modern is good because it has an "identity," because it respects "the human scale," because it establishes a relationship with "history," because it relates to its "context," and so on) betray an unfulfilled longing—and thus a deficiency—in contemporary society.

What we have here is an oppositional mechanism of quite extraordinary persuasiveness. It works by negating reality and creating an alternative whose characteristics have more to do with the world of desires. Consider the oft-stated "truths" compared to real-world conditions: Post-Modern skyscrapers relate to their context (in reality they are used as advertising images and therefore aim precisely to stand out); Post-Modern skyscrapers respect the human scale (in reality they are bigger and taller than their predecessors); Post-Modern skyscrapers establish a relationship with history (actually they are a prime example of nonconsideration of history). This mechanism reflects a unique feature of contemporary society: an unconscious parallelism between the world of fantasy and that of reality. And if the real world belongs to business, the world of fantasy is the realm of architects.

But the claims of Post-Modern theory also supply a vital point of reference: they create something in the void, delineate a boundary

53rd Street at Third Avenue, New York, 1986, John Burgee Architects with Philip Johnson. (Photo: Dida Biggi)

that acts as a support. Post-Modernism's function may be compared to that of the planner's graph paper on which the new city takes shape, upon which the skyscraper's facade is drawn. There is no time to reflect or analyze, nor, perhaps, any desire to do so. What is needed, therefore, is a ready-made, easily acceptable and repeatable theory, one that allows everyone to get on with the job. From the point of view of production, this theory works: it got the skyscraper construction market going again, or at least it coincided with this phenomenon, and is therefore acceptable and valid.

It should be borne in mind that this theory, with production as its prime object, is not founded on reality but rather on how reality is desired to be. On a functional human level, the behavior pattern may be charming enough in children, where the borderline between the worlds of reality and fantasy may be tenuous, but for the adult this mechanism—the retreat into an imaginary world—is called delirium. In a state of delirium reality is superceded by an imaginary world. In order for this mechanism to be triggered humans must find themselves facing an unacceptable reality. From the European standpoint, Americans, with only 200 years of history, are a people in their infancy, and as such, Post-Modern theory constitutes without doubt a retreat from an unacceptable reality into the world of fantasy. Such a retreat, when it lasts a limited amount of time, may be a normal phenomenon, forming part of a process of growth and maturation. Somewhat more worrisome is that the illusion is encouraged in the United States because business has found it to be a veritable gold mine.

ARCHITECTS AND POWER

The strong reaction against International style skyscrapers seems neither heartfelt nor very sincere. We are left with the impression that architects who criticize them are not altogether conscious of what they are doing. It is as if they were venting their anger on something that in reality does not exist.

In the first place, the antagonism shows up on a formal level alone. No one questions the actual significance of Modern architecture, why it took the forms it did, or what economic, historic, or political factors determined it. Forgotten in considering the architecture of the past is what the architecture of the present continually makes clear: the importance of reality in the construction of a skyscraper and the importance of the developer in deciding its form (the Chrysler Building's famous top was the express wish of the developer and not of the architect, Van Alen).[31] To ignore the economic and market forces that shaped a skyscraper is to ignore reality. Yet architects, and above all those involved in designing skyscrapers, come up against this reality every single day. Twenty years ago it was no different. So is it actually true that architects have all this power? Is it not rather the case that the architects of skyscrapers face an economic reality with very precise and not readily alterable rules?

The assault on International style skyscrapers may also be read in another way: as an attempt to assign to architects a measure of power that they actually do not have. To blame the architects of the 1960s is to attribute to them a power they never had. They too had to come to terms with the laws of the reality in which skyscrapers are rooted. The architect of skyscrapers does not create spaces. He uses, with a few variations of his own, spaces that already have been defined. The only freedom allowed the architect (and even this is limited) in the final analysis has to do with the skyscraper's image. Having lost his power over space, the architect has become a designer. Perhaps in attacking the International style, architects are expressing a desire to recapture the space that they feel has somehow been denied them. Yet in this way—deluding themselves that they possess a power that they do not, satisfying real wants on the level of illusion— they have not the slightest possibility of bringing about any change in reality and, therefore, of building true spaces.

In foreground: One South Wacker building, Chicago, 1984, Murphy/Jahn
Architects. (Photo: Murphy/Jahn Architects)

Hercules Inc. headquarters, Wilmington, Del., 1983, Kohn Pedersen Fox
Associates. (Photo © 1983 Norman McGrath, ASMP)

SENTIMENTAL REEDUCATION

The New York Image

Canaletto's painting of an imaginary Venice may be considered to be one of the first advertising images of the modern era. A view of Palladian structures, including a design for the new Rialto bridge (never built), extended an invitation to the legendary eighteenth-century travelers who journeyed to Italy on the Grand Tour.

Like Canaletto's fantastic representation of Venice, New York's image is also used as a promotional device. But it is no longer confined simply to inviting tourists to undertake trips abroad. Having acquired power on a far vaster economic plane, New York's image continues to serve as an invitation, but for the most diverse proposals: to invest in a construction company, to buy a particular liquor or brand of cigarettes, a computer, or a television.

The message is no longer direct, as might be the message in a landscape image inviting people to travel somewhere; it has become

Capriccio Con Edifici Palladiani: painting by Canaletto. (Courtesy Archivio Sopraintendenza per i Beni Artistici e Storici per le province di Parma e Piacenza)

Philips advertisement showing fantasy
of a Manhattan skyline in a light bulb.
(Courtesy ATA Belier S.P.A.)

more complex. The power of attraction exercised by New York's
image is due to what that image (or the very name of New York)
has begun to represent, to symbolize for our society.

Human beings have a tendency to project their internal state of
being onto the outside world, and, by the same principle, to identify
aspects of themselves in the city in which they live or aspire to live.
New York is beautiful as an image—grandiose and exciting. The same
cannot be said of her spaces. Her architecture is directed primarily
toward the sense of sight, and, more generally, toward the world of
illusion, of imagination. New York is the ideal city for people's
dreams, more so than for people as they actually are. New York
reflects the mentality of the world of which it is a part—a world
that considers only certain aspects of human beings (such as productivity or capacity for consumption) and not their complexity and

PPG Place, Pittsburgh, 1983,
Johnson/Burgee Architects. (Photo:
Richard Payne)

entirety. Illusion plays a fundamental role in this. In fact it is through the use of illusion that people can be brought to manifest determined behavior patterns—to be productive, to consume. There is no doubt that a person who is considered solely on the basis of (or, worse, as the sum of) these characteristics can only be unhappy with reality and thus easy prey to illusions.

Image and Space

A deep rift exists between appearance and content in the skyscraper because the skyscraper's exterior contains no clue to its interior: its form says nothing of the skyscraper as a spatial entity.

This separation of image from space in the skyscraper suggests that there is a division in our perception of architecture: architecture is felt as space and perceived as image, an enormous three-dimensional image. In the skyscraper, space and form (or rather image) are not melded—they are stuck together.

At this point we might note how International style skyscrapers express, perhaps more than any other form, the dichotomy between image and space. Their elementary, parallelepipedal glass forms express the very opposite of the fragmented and tense lifestyle that characterizes the skyscraper's interior space. In the International style skyscraper, the contrast between image and interior space is emphasized, taken to the extreme. It may be likened to a contrast between immobility and movement, grandiosity and fragmentation.

To look at it, the skyscraper seems powerful and immobile, grandiose and static, while inside all is nervous and active, fragmented and frantic. Perhaps it is for this reason that the sensations felt at sidewalk level in New York are so different from those aroused by gazing at the profile of the Wall Street skyscrapers. Contrasting against the strength and immobility of New York's image is a tumultuous, fragmented space of crowds, speed, automobiles, movement, and a barrage of billboards.

Sentimental Reeducation

In *Collage City* Colin Rowe affirms the rift between the skyscraper's internal activity and its external appearance. If we think of the skyscraper as a representation (or, at least, a representational manifestation) of the human mind, then this rift corresponds to the need to keep separate the spheres of reality and fantasy. This is just what happens at Disney World, where technology is carefully hidden so that fantasy may become reality, where:

> *several hundred acres of mostly fiberglass fantasy rest upon an unseen technological substructure without earthly parallel, where, with easy access and accommodating all the vast priorities of change, are contained all the required services—vacuum garbage systems, electrical circuitry, sewage*

PPG Place, Pittsburgh, as shown in a PTI Sealants advertisement.

lines, complete supply tractor traffic routes and total behind (or below) the scenes access for the costumed employees who fuel the various theatres of illusion above: and it should be evident that the correct analogy is that of the New York skyscraper: on the 65th floor is the Rainbow Room where the consumption of Transcendentalist cocktails is the order of the day and then, way, way beneath (out of sight but not out of mind) is the pragmatic sub-basement, which facilitates both the upstairs afflatus and public euphoria. In both cases the two worlds of illusion and fact, of publicity and privacy, are insulated. Inter-dependent but separate, they may possibly be equal, but in no way are they to be integrated.[32]

Rowe interprets this phenomenon as a need on the part of society to keep the world of fantasy separate from that of reality. Moreover, the two worlds are mutually exclusive: euphoria and enjoyment can exist only if reality is hidden from view, forgotten, canceled. What is looked for in fantasy is a reality purified of all unpleasant and painful aspects. Happiness can only be reached through illusion.

In *Delirious New York* Rem Koolhaas also speaks of a schism in the skyscraper. Here the antithesis is in regard to internal and external space. According to Koolhaas, the reason for this rift can be found in the need to spare the outside world from the torment within:

In the deliberate discrepancy between container and contained New York's makers discover an area of unprecedented freedom. They exploit and formalize it in the architectural equivalent of a lobotomy—the surgical severance of the connection between the frontal lobes and the rest of the brain to relieve some mental disorders by disconnecting thought processes from emotions.

The architectural equivalent separates exterior and interior architecture. In this way the Monolith spares the outside world the agonies of the continuous changes raging inside it. It hides everyday life.[33]

In *Space, Time and Architecture*, Siegfried Giedion writes that the contemporary human being is characterized by a schism between the worlds of intellect and feeling. Feelings, contrary to intellectual capacities, have atrophied and Giedion sees some sort of sentimental reeducation as the only remedy for such a situation. He arrives at this conclusion through a study not of the skyscraper, but of the parkway, and highlights the difference of scale between parkway and *rue corridor*. The same difference of scale separates thought from feeling. It is only in those moments in which thoughts and feelings coexisted in a "balanced relationship" that man has created civilizations that can be called great from every point of view. As examples, he cites the Athens of Pericles, and the Rome of Augustus.[34]

NOTES

1. K. T. Gibbs, *Business Architectural Imagery in America 1870–1930* (Ann Arbor: University of Michigan Press, 1985).

2. U. Eco, *La Struttura Assente (The Absent Structure)* (Milan: Gruppo Editoriale Fabbri Bompiani Sonzogno Etas S.P.A., 1983), 169.

3. S. Diamond, *The Reputation of the American Businessman* (Cambridge, MA: Harvard University Press, 1966), 103. Reprinted by permission of the publishers. Copyright © 1955 by the President and Fellows of Harvard College, copyright © 1983 by Sigmund Oscar Diamond.

4. K. Lorenz, *Civilized Man's Eight Deadly Sins* (Orlando, FL; Harcourt Brace Jovanovich). Copyright © 1973 by R. Piper and Company Verlag, English translation copyright © 1974 by Konrad Lorenz, reprinted by permission of Harcourt Brace Jovanovich, Inc.

5. Lever House was recently designated as a landmark, thus saving it from demolition. The firm of Swanke, Hayden & Connel Architects had already drawn up plans for a Post-Modern skyscraper, four times as large, to take its place.

6. G. M. Anderson, "Kohn, Pederson, Fox: External Forces Shape Multiform Towers," *Architectural Record*, June 1981, 81. Copyright 1981 by McGraw-Hill, Inc. All rights reserved. Reproduced with the permission of the publisher.

7. P. Goldberger, "A Homage to the Skyscraper," *The New York Times*, 18 April 1981. Copyright © 1982 by The New York Times Company. Reprinted by permission.

8. T. Hine, "Architects Build Quick Success." From *The Philadelphia Inquirer*, 15 July 1982, used by permission.

9. P. Goldberger, "Chicago Has a New Profile," *The New York Times*, 8 May 1983. Copyright © 1983 by The New York Times Company. Reprinted by permission.

10. W. Wagner, Jr., "Something Big Is Happening in a Big Hurry in the Design of Those Big Office Towers," *Architectural Record*, June 1981, 13. Copyright 1981 by McGraw-Hill, Inc. All rights reserved. Reproduced with the permission of the publisher.

11. P. Viladas, "Gothic Romance," *Progressive Architecture*, February 1984, 86, 88, 93.

12. P. Goldberger, *The Skyscraper* (New York: Alfred A. Knopf, 1989), 139–40:

By 1980, one thing was clear: the box, the rationalist dream of the International Style, was making more and more architects uncomfortable. Not only was it no longer the clean and exhilarating structure that would serve as a clarion call to a new age, but it was not even able to hold out much promise of practicality. It was generally inefficient from the standpoint of energy, and it was not as marketable from the viewpoint of real estate operators either.

For by the end of the 1970s, the success of a few notable skyscrapers of the previous decade, buildings like IDS and Pennzoil Place and Citicorp Center and

John Hancock Tower, had led clients to become increasingly receptive to alternatives to the austere glass box. John Portma's projects, too, had played a role in changing public tastes—and hence market demands—toward skyscrapers that would provide occasions for social interaction, that would act as enclosed public meeting places, town squares, agoras *of a sort, and not merely house offices or hotel rooms or identical apartment units. At the end of 1980 most of the large skyscrapers under construction in New York City contained at least some sort of public atrium, retail mall, or "galleria," as it has become common to call such places, and that alone distinguished the new group of buildings from its predecessors, Third Avenue's banal 1960s glass boxes.*

And at least one building of a previous generation, the 277 Park Avenue tower by Emery Roth and Sons of 1963, was being renovated by Haines, Lundberg, Waehler to include a glass-enclosed public atrium in the space in front of the building previously occupied by an austere concrete plaza. The renovation was at the request of the building's major tenant, Chemical Bank, which insisted on (and agreed to pay for) a means by which the tower could be given public identification. The bank's recognition that 277 Park Avenue in its original form lacked such identification and its decision to try, however awkwardly, to turn the building into something resembling later skyscrapers, ranks as a final admission by the most conservative of clients that the corporate style of the 1950s no longer suited its needs.

So just as it had been economics, and not esthetics, that had ultimately won the battle of modernism after World War II, it was economics of a sort that turned buildings away from the Miesian boxes with which they had been filling American cities since the mid-1950s. The revolution that modernism represented had been won, after all, in corporate boardrooms in the 1950s, not in European design studios in the 1920s. And the events occurring in those same boardrooms in the late 1970s and early 1980s suggest the victory of modernism, while broad, was not particularly deep.

13. "Architecture as a Corporate Asset," *Business Week*, 4 October 1982, 125.

14. *Ibid.*

15. *Ibid.*

16. As quoted by W. C. Clark and J. L. Kingston, *The Skyscraper: A Study in the Economic Height of Modern Office Building* (New York and Cleveland: American Institute of Steel Construction, 1930), 79–80.

17. T. J. Peters and R. H. Waterman, Jr., *In Search of Excellence* (New York: Harpur & Row). Copyright © 1982 by Thomas J. Peters and Robert H. Waterman, Jr. Reprinted by permission Harpur & Row, Publishers, Inc.

18. R. Arnheim, *Visual Thinking* (Berkeley: University of California Press), 1980, 136–37. Copyright © 1969 The Regents of the University of California.

19. *Ibid.*, 175.

The extent of the shift in architecture toward a business rather than a professional identity is difficult to quantify, since what most architects have been doing is altering their approach gradually, not abandoning traditional concerns altogether.

Philip Johnson, for example, long considered a pure esthetician, has been working in close tandem with real-estate developers in recent years "because it's the only way to get things built today," he says.

He says that he still considers himself a designer foremost, but he now searches for ways to make esthetic statements economically viable.

20. Goldberger, *The Skyscraper,* 124.

21. P. Goldberger, "Architects Widen Traditional Role to Give Clients Business Service," *The New York Times,* 4 January 1977. Copyright © 1977 by The New York Times Company. Reprinted by permission:

The extent of the shift in architecture toward a business rather than a professional identity is difficult to quantify, since what most architects have been doing is altering their approach gradually, not abandoning traditional concerns altogether.

Philip Johnson, for example, long considered a pure esthetician, has been working in close tandem with real-estate developers in recent years "because it's the only way to get things built today," he says.

He says that he still considers himself a designer foremost, but he now searches for ways to make esthetic statements economically viable.

22. Peters and Waterman, 26.

23. P. Letarouilly, *Edifices de la Rome Moderne ou Recueil des Palais, Maisons, Eglises et Autres Monuments . . .* (Paris: Didot, 1840).

24. C. Rowe, *Collage City* (Cambridge, MA: MIT Press, 1978) 172.

25. Letarouilly, *Les Batiments du Vatican* (London: Tiranti, 1963).

26. Rowe, 151.

27. *Ibid.,* 144–45.

28. Eco, 214–15.

29. K. Lynch, *What's Time Is This Place?* (Cambridge, MA: MIT Press, 1972), *passim.*

30. For example, the following excerpt relates to the Hercules Inc. building, designed by Kohn Pederson Fox Associates and built in Wilmington, Delaware in 1983: ". . . [T]he base is designed to reduce the effect of bulk and create a recognizably human scale . . ." From "Wilmington: A Stone Base Tames the Impact of a Green Glass Cube," *Architectural Record,* June 1981, 86.

31. R. Koolhaas, *Delirious New York* (New York: Oxford University Press, 1978), 45.

32. Rowe, 44–45.

33. Koolhaas, p. 98

34. S. Giedion, *Space, Time and Architecture* (Cambridge, MA: Harvard University Press, 1967), *passim.*

The Bank of Southwest competition:
winning entry (rendering), Houston,
1982, Murphy/Jahn Architects.
(Courtesy Murphy/Jahn Architects)

Citicorp Center, as shown in a mid-1980s Citibank brochure, New York. (Courtesy Citicorp)

Photo montage of downtown Manhattan: The World Financial Center (foreground),
1987, Cesar Pelli & Associates; the World Trade Center (behind), Minoru Yamasaki;
the Woolworth Building (background at left), 1913, Cass Gilbert. (Photo: Wolfgang
Hoyt)

Above—900 North Michigan Avenue: model, Chicago, 1988, Kohn Pedersen Fox
Associates. (Photo: Jack Horner)

Left—The first Post-Modern skyscraper: the American Telephone & Telegraph
corporate headquarters (arched base), New York, 1985, Johnson/Burgee Architects.
(Photo: Richard Payne)

Facing page—125 East 57th Street: plexiglass model showing shape and facade, New York, 1988, Kohn Pedersen Fox Associates. (Photo: Jack Horner)

Right—Top of Citicorp Center, as shown in Delta advertisement, New York. (Courtesy Delta Faucet Company, Indianapolis, IN)

Below—900 North Michigan Avenue: model of a shop at base of the tower, Chicago, 1988, Kohn Pedersen Fox Associates. (Photo: Jock Pottle)

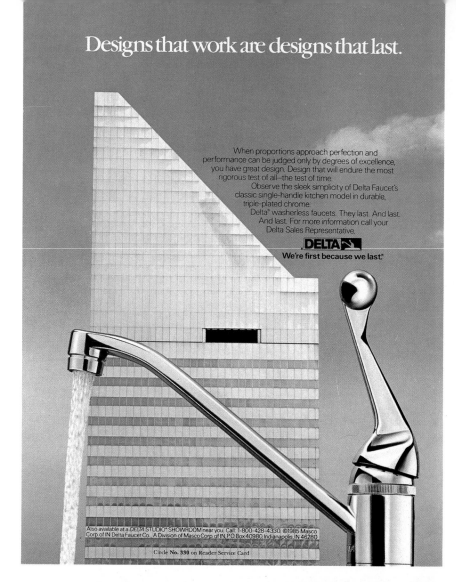

Above—125 East 57th Street: paper model showing the building's facade, New York, 1988, Kohn Pedersen Fox Associates. (Photo: Jock Pottle)

Left—125 East 57th Street: plexiglass model showing building's shape, New York, 1988, Kohn Pedersen Fox Associates. (Photo: Jock Pottle)

Above—900 North Michigan Avenue: model of the lobby, Chicago, 1988, Kohn Pedersen Fox Associates. (Photo: Jock Pottle)

Right—The New York skyline, as depicted in an advertisement with a bottle of Grand Marnier. (Courtesy Carillon Importers Ltd.; artist: Isadore Seltzer)

Above—International Paper headquarters: staircase, New York, 1983, The Space Design Group. (Photo: Mark Ross)

Right—Executive office furniture in Henredon Furniture Industries advertisement. (Courtesy Henredon Furniture Industries, Inc., Morganton, NC)

National Westminster Bank USA: general offices, New York, 1984, The Space Design Group. (Photo: Mark Ross)

Chemical Bank headquarters: boardroom, New York, 1982, Haines Lundberg
Waehler. (Photo: © Peter Aaron/Esto)

McDonald's headquarters: think tank, interior view, Chicago, 1973, Associated Space Design. (Courtesy Associated Space Design)

2

The Models

REPRESENTATIONAL TECHNIQUES

Plans, facades and sections, clay models, photographs, cinematography: these are our methods of representing spaces. Once the sense of the architecture has been put across, each one of these methods may be investigated, examined closely, improved; each makes its own original contribution, while its lacunae are compensated for by the others. If, as the cubists believed, architecture may be defined in four dimensions, we would have adequate means for a complete representation of spaces.

. . . Cinematography may portray one, two, three possible paths for the observer in space, but space is perceived by an infinite number of paths.[1]

In this chapter, the Post-Modern skyscraper is analyzed by means of the models used by architects during various planning stages. Representational techniques are a precious source of information, for as well as representing the object, they also show how humans represent it internally, and therefore how they perceive, feel, and imagine it. In other words, representational techniques reveal the relationship between humans and the object to be represented. As we shall see, the models used in the planning of skyscrapers reveal several aspects of the people that build them and that live and work inside them.

In planning a skyscraper's form and facade, one particular representational technique prevails—the model. Naturally, sketches, plans, sections, elevations, and so on, are also made, but it is the model, more than any drawing, that most seems to satisfy representational requirements.

Raymond Hood, Wallace K. Harrison, and Andrew Reinhard with model of La Maison Française and British Empire Building, now flanking the Channel Gardens in Rockefeller Center, New York. (Photo courtesy of Rockefeller Center, © Rockefeller Group, Inc.)

Developers Robert V. Tishman and Jerry I. Speyer appear with a model of the Continental Illinois building, New York. (Photo: Rob Knot)

John Wiegman poses with a model of One Westheimer Plaza, Houston, in a 1979 advertisement for Morris*Aubrey Architects. (Courtesy Marshall Pengra, Inc. advertising agency)

The importance of models in planning skyscrapers cannot help but remind us of the importance that models have acquired in contemporary science. Since we no longer believe in the possibility of knowing the truth, we recognize that our knowledge is humble and transitory, consisting of nothing more than models of reality that we have constructed in our minds. It goes without saying that such models are of the utmost value, yet they are fated to represent only intermediate stages in our advancing journey toward knowledge.

Facing page—Models of 900 North Michigan Avenue, lobby, Chicago, 1988, Kohn Pedersen Fox Associates. (Photos: Jock Pottle)

Right—Model of 900 North Michigan Avenue, Chicago, 1988, Kohn Pedersen Fox Associates. (Photo: Jack Horner)

The Model and the Skyscraper

Facing page and below—Models of 900 North Michigan Avenue, top of building, Chicago, 1988, Kohn Pedersen Fox Associates. (Photos: Jock Pottle)

The skyscraper's form and facade are designed by means of a series of models of different sizes made out of various materials. Both paper and plasticine models (so-called *progressive models*) are used in various planning stages. A clay model is used for rapidly molding the form that the skyscraper will take; a paper model lends itself to the assem-

bly and collage techniques adopted in the design of the facade. Plexiglass models serve to crystallize each satisfactory solution arrived at during the process, and also, of course, the definitive version of the whole.

The model's scale and the materials from which it is made vary according to the requirements of each phase of work. In deciding the skyscraper's general shape a small scale is used; the scale then

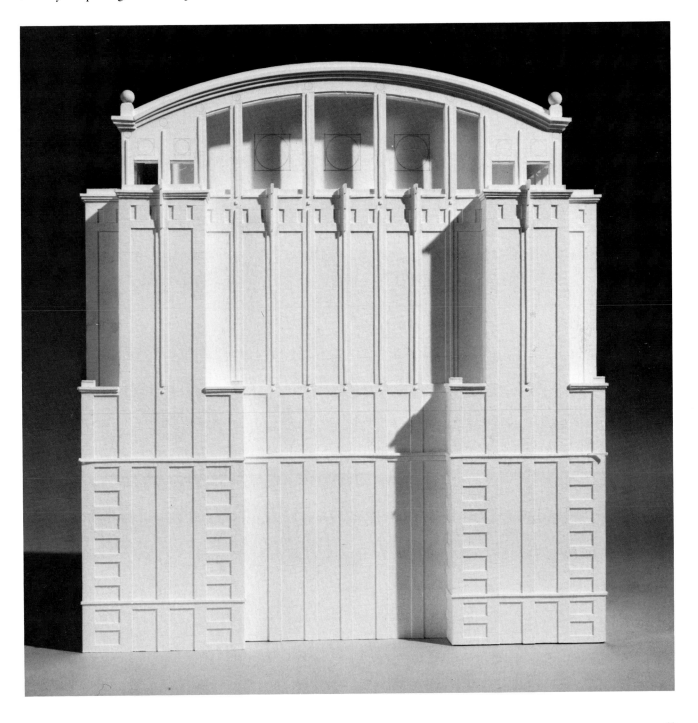

increases stage by stage, to the point where life-size models of certain decorative details may be executed. The model increases in size and detail as ideas for the skyscraper's appearance are finalized.

The model is not only an instrument for controlling the architect's ideas; it is also the means by which the architect comes to refine and solidify those ideas.

The Clay Model

The photographs accompanying this chapter include a series of models used by the firm of Kohn Pedersen Fox Associates of New York in the planning of three skyscrapers designed for Chicago, Pittsburgh, and New York, respectively.

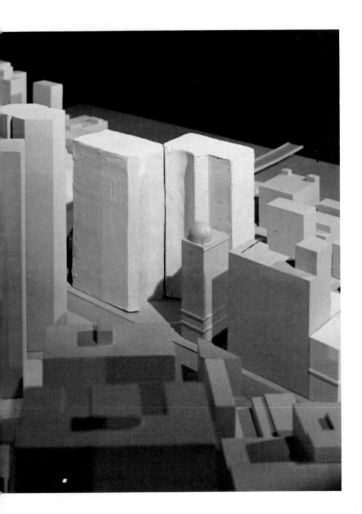

Allegheny International Building: clay models showing several planning stages of the form of the twin skyscrapers, Pittsburgh, 1987, Kohn Pedersen Fox Associates. (Photos: Jock Pottle)

Clay's soft, pliable properties make it an ideal material for rapidly molding the skyscraper's form and for controlling its effect in the urban panorama, the latter also reproduced in the studio by a small-scale plexiglass model (also known as a site model). By reproducing the skyscraper's mass on a scale that will not overwhelm human eyes, the clay model allows the architect to control whatever effects may be produced by other forms in the physical context in which the skyscraper is to be introduced.

By drastically reducing the field of imagination, the clay model and the site model offer something concrete from which to work, providing a base and setting limits. This phase of planning is particularly concerned with problems of volumes, masses, and points of view. The model allows all factors to be taken into account, each ele-

ment to be concretely visible, every piece of information to be re-produced in a few square feet of space: the skyscraper's volume, the volumes already existent in the surrounding spaces, the principal points of view. The drastic reduction of scale proves nonetheless to be extremely stimulating, for while the field of imagination is restricted and solidified by means of the model, at the same time the imagination has room to range freely within the bounds set for it.

By bending down and half closing one's eyes, it is possible to control the volumetric arrangement of existing buildings and the principal points of view from which the skyscraper will be seen. Each piece of the problem is solidified by the model's "realness" and con-

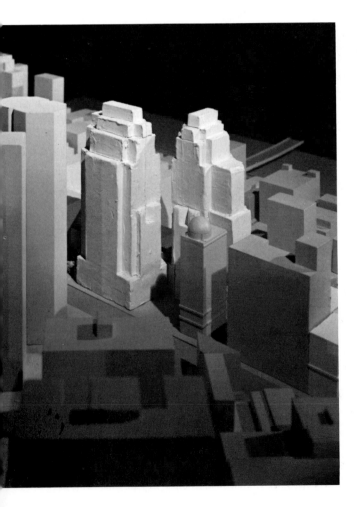 

Allegheny International Building: clay models showing several planning stages of the form of the twin skyscrapers, Pittsburgh, 1987, Kohn Pedersen Fox Associates. (Photos: Jock Pottle)

creteness and is made clearly visible by the dark gray of the plexiglass that forms the background and by the soft, light-colored mass of clay that represents the skyscraper. Once all the known factors have been taken into account, the possible design solutions are, of course, infinite: twin towers with a circular piazza in the center; twin towers with quadrangular piazza; two differently shaped towers; and so on. Experiment after experiment is carried out until the table is covered with models, creating a miniature city. All possibilities and variations are examined, while the miniature city slowly spreads itself out upon the table. At last, the form is decided upon and a plexiglass model is made.

The Paper Model

At the stage of facade design, paper is used to make a light, strong model that is easily cut and pasted. The facade is glued onto the skyscraper's silhouette in the same way that the panels of glass or limestone will later be hooked onto the skyscraper's exterior structure.

Once the facade is glued on, its effect on the paper model is assessed. Then the experiments begin: first one top is tried on, then another; the tower base is varied; then the window groupings destroyed and rebuilt from scratch;—the model continually renewed. All the possible variations are tried until a satisfactory one is found. In the end, a very carefully built and very expensive plexiglass model crystallizes the chosen solution.

Advantages and Disadvantages

The model offers several advantages, given the planning method used to define the skyscraper's external appearance. It can be made very quickly, it stimulates the imagination, and it is eminently suited to the trial-and-error method of working, in that it permits the rapid elaboration of various forms (or facades) and their immediate verification or rejection. It lends itself, better than drawing, to the marketing operations that accompany the planning of the skyscraper. Also, and no less importantly, the model protects architects from the gigantic scale of the projects they carry out.

Above and pages 66 and 67— Allegheny International Building: models showing both towers in nearly finished form, with final touches, Pittsburgh, 1987, Kohn Pedersen Fox Associates. (Photos © Dan Cornish/ Esto)

Facing page— Allegheny International Building: Plexiglas models showing changes during design, Pittsburgh, 1987, Kohn Pedersen Fox Associates. (Photos: Jack Horner)

Yet, being a tool of illusion, the model has a further characteristic that may turn out to be a danger for the architect. Because the model is a representational technique that is more realistic than others, it may create the illusion of being more faithful than it really is. The model's greatest strength is, ironically, its greatest weakness. The architect, concentrating all attention on the model, may well be led to forget a fundamental characteristic of architecture: its spatial context.

Compensatory Gratification

Among the Woolworth Building's ornamental friezes is a bas-relief portraying Cass Gilbert holding a model of his skyscraper. The January 1979 cover of *Time* shows Philip Johnson in the same pose with a model of the AT&T. These two images reveal an inter-

esting aspect of the relationship between the architects of skyscrapers and their plans. The architects' pose expresses possessiveness and dominion rather than affection. It reveals a desire to dominate, all the more urgent because it is unsatisfied—the desire to be the master (father) of one's own work. The model seems to satisfy a need that the finished architectural work—the skyscraper—denies.

Scale Reduction

The model ignores a fundamental parameter—the human parameter. While it may effectively demonstrate the relationships between the building's separate parts, it does not take into account the point of view, in the literal sense of the term, of the human being. However, in certain circumstances this deficiency may be an asset: it may be useful in situations where the human parameter must not taken into account.

There is one characteristic of the model that becomes interesting above all if one considers that it is used to represent skyscrapers. The model, unlike the drawing, represents the architectural work in three dimensions. The drawing, on the other hand, although using a similar reduction of scale, preserves along with its two-dimensionality the ability to re-create the effect that a building of gigantic dimensions produces on human beings. (It is enough to remember Hugh Ferriss's low-perspective drawings of the New York zoning laws in 1916.)

The most shocking feature of the skyscraper is its height—the very feature that the model attenuates. That the architect planning a skyscraper makes use of a representational technique that cancels out its principal effect has to be significant. The following hypothesis may perhaps be formulated: in shrinking the skyscraper's dimensions, the model restores to the architect's dominion something that in reality has escaped him. It is almost as if skyscrapers are too big to be imaginable and have to have small-scale models made of them in order to be introduced to us. (This would mean that it is not the skyscraper that is imagined, but its model, an enlargement of which will *become* the skyscraper.) We might therefore ask ourselves whether the model is meant to serve the architect, the client who has commissioned it, or the general public; and whether it serves before or after the project has been realized.

The Model and Imagination

The model opens the way to discussion of a very important subject: the imagination, a subject that takes in the whole range of representational techniques. Obviously, imagination inhabits an internal, mental space. What sort of relationship exists between this space and reality? How does something that is still being planned, that does not yet exist in reality, represent itself to us? Representational techniques are fundamental in the architect's work, in that the space (or form) created is a space (or form) that has begun its life inside the architect. We might say that the representational technique is a sort of bridge between the world of the imagination and that of reality, a means by which an imagined space may be transformed, step by step, into a real space.

The model not only allows this first materialization of the imagination; it is also a precious stimulus. The drastic reduction of scale in the construction of a model is already a passage into the world of the imagination. In reducing the skyscraper's size, the model also carries out a kind of demystification of the skyscraper's gigantic proportions—an aspect that is among the most difficult to come to terms with, arouses the most fears, and causes the most problems. Thanks to the model, the architect is relieved of the problems that might result from perfect awareness of what is being planned.

Portrait of Cass Gilbert in an ornamental frieze in the lobby of the Woolworth Building, New York.

The primary function of the model, then, seems to be stimulating the imagination. The model is nothing but a fantasy that has been realized, one destined to become redundant for the very reason that it has been realized.

Ephemeral Giants

The models used by architects in the fifteenth and sixteenth centuries, while very beautiful in their coarse wooden simplicity, were imprecise because they referred to something bigger: they were merely rough sketches of how finished work would look. It is out of the question to think anything can take the place of St. Peter's; it is a unique work. The same cannot be said for a skyscraper, a work that is likewise on a huge scale but at the same time easily replaceable. The architect planning a skyscraper has to deal with an architectural work of gigantic proportions, while knowing full well that it may be short-lived. Although the skyscraper is an architectural prodigy, it is also an ephemeral form of architecture. Far from eternal, the architecture of our time may not even be allowed to age by a century. We no longer build pyramids, churches, or castles but skyscrapers that, despite their enormous proportions, are temporary and easily expendable. The constructed work has become less enduring while its model has become less ephemeral.

Seduction

Models are used by architectural firms not only for their representational properties but also as effective publicity tools. Newspapers more frequently publish photographs of models than of the finished buildings. The various stages in planning a skyscraper's appearance—its form, its facade, its decorative details—are shown to clients in the form of models. By looking at a model, clients are able to gain a better understanding of how the design is proceeding, and, above all, they are likely to be seduced.

The model lends itself well to the marketing operations that accompany the planning of the skyscraper, in that a model is a seductive object in itself. Architects presenting the press—and therefore the public—and the client with models of their projects (models, it should be noted, that are excellently produced and finely finished) clearly intend to seduce: in presenting these delightful objects architects attempt to win approval for their work. Their clients, the developers, are similarly intentioned when they present skyscraper models to banks in order to get loans, and to potential tenants in order to rent or sell space. The technique of seducing the client through imagination, or more generally through illusion, is, of course, a technique used by businessmen every day.

Prefiguration

That photographs of models are published in newspapers and that developers use these models to sell office space tells us that a further process is underway: the prefiguration of reality created by the model evidently has the power to speed up the pace of skyscraper business. No need to wait for the skyscraper to be built—business can be transacted around the model. Models and photomontages (which, by incorporating the photo of the model, reproduce a future or hypothetical reality) offer the possibility of working on a model of reality rather than reality itself and have the advantage of prefiguring and anticipating it.

The Photomontage

By facilitating the creation of architectural photomontages, the model may prefigure reality so realistically as to be often indistinguishable from it. A photograph of the model stands in for the finished building. In the illusion created by the photomontage, the image and the object seem to proclaim their victory over space (and of illusion over reality).

This theme seems inseparable from the world of the skyscraper. The clash of reality and illusion, of image and space, is encountered again and again. Yet, more than a clash, it might be defined as a genuine attempt on the part of the world of imagination and illusion (which technology continually strengthens) to take the place of reality.

Simulation: More Real than Reality

The reality of the future is ably simulated in the photomontage. By making the photo look realistic, technology is able to give form to something that belongs to the world of fantasy. The same principle can be seen at work in science fiction films, where special effects make things appear so lifelike that they seem real. Or again, at Disney World, where an extremely refined and cleverly concealed technological apparatus manages to render the world of fantasy real (as in the haunted house, where laser beams compose transparent, three-dimensional images—holograms—that appear to dance in mid-air). Here at Disney World, as in the photographic studios commissioned to work for architects, technology is used to make illusion real. Yet these continued attempts by the world of imagination and illusion to substitute their images for reality are indicative of how strong, uncompromising, and difficult that reality must be.

The Bank of Southwest competition: model, Houston, 1982, Kohn Pedersen Fox Associates. (Photo: Jack Horner)

The Bank of Southwest competition: second prize, Houston, 1982, Kohn Pedersen
Fox Associates. (Photo: Jack Horner)

An American version of Venice at
Disney World, Orlando, Fla. (Photo:
Dida Biggi)

A French castle at Disney World,
Orlando, Fla. (Photo: Dida Biggi)

Above—A Western view of China at Disney World, Orlando, Fla. (Photo: Dida Biggi)

A "tropical isle" at Disney World, Orlando, Fla. (Photo: Dida Biggi)

MINIATURIZATION

A Comparison

A comparison between Hugh Ferriss's 1922 drawings for New York's zoning law and the skyscraper models presently in use by American architectural firms shows two quite different conceptions of the skyscraper. Ferriss's drawings emphasize the skyscrapers' grandiose and vertical qualities: they appear as enormous, gloomy, severe masses that soar upward from extremely solid bases, becoming progressively narrower as they climb toward the sky. In Ferriss's conception, sky-

Study for the maximum mass permitted by the 1922 New York Zoning Law, Stage 4, by Hugh Ferriss, 1922. (Photo: Scott Hyde; Courtesy the Cooper-Hewitt Museum, Smithsonian Institution/Art Resource, New York)

scrapers are giants that inspire fear, and the city, which takes on their form, appears magnificent, powerful, lugubrious. Humans are but tiny shadows compared with such greatness. It is impossible to imagine that humans have been responsible for constructing these giants.

Models, by comparison, do not celebrate the skyscraper's grandiosity; in fact they do just the opposite. The skyscraper is lowered, made smaller—despite the fact that today's skyscrapers are much higher than their predecessors. The fearsome giant is transformed into an attractive object. The model is either photographed from above, or frontally, as it would appear from the twenty-fifth floor of a neighboring skyscraper.

Allegheny International Building: model of both towers, Pittsburgh, 1987, Kohn Pedersen Fox Associates. (Photo: Jack Horner)

In the former case, Ferriss's drawings, the skyscraper is a giant that inspires fear; in the latter, as a model, it is a pleasing object. In the former, it is rendered in dark tints; in the latter, there is an abundance of color, including pinks and sky-blues. The skyscraper's verticality, once exalted, is now deformed. It is Ferriss's drawings that more adequately describe our perception of reality, whether the skyscraper is observed from the street, from a nearby skyscraper, or from the windows of a helicopter.

In Ferriss's renderings, humans opt for an external rather than internal grandeur, as if desirous of a God or a father. In the case of models or their photographs, all sense of grandeur has disappeared.

Architectural Miniatures

Let me here add a consideration which seems to me to be absolutely pertinent: the exhibition of models which are colored, or which have been made attractive by painting clearly indicates that the architect does not seek simply to represent his plan, but that his ambition leads him to try to attract the eye of the onlooker superficially, to fill it with wonder, and to distract the spirit from an attentive and reflective examination of the model's various parts. We should therefore avoid making models which are perfectly finished or decorated and striking: it is better to make them unadorned, so that it is the perfection of the conception, and not the skill of execution which is demonstrated. For it is here that the real difference between the work of the painter and that of the architect lies: the former attempts on canvas to depict objects in relief by means of shadows and diminishing lines and angles; the architect, on the contrary, avoids shadows and represents relief by means of the design of his plan, showing in other designs the form and the extension of each facade and each side by making use of real corners and unvariable lines: he proceeds as if he desired that his work not be judged on the basis of illusory appearances, but on the contrary, evaluated exactly on the basis of controllable measures.[2]

What strikes us above all when reading this fragment of *De re aedificatoria* and examining photographs of present-day scale models is how the latter manifest the very characteristics that Alberti recommends avoiding in the construction of an architectural model—that is, an excessive indulgence in "illusory appearances." This different way of considering models corresponds to a different conception of architecture. It must be said that, over the course of the centuries, the illusory techniques that Alberti regarded as tools of the painter alone have become fundamental to the work of the architect as well. But what is particularly interesting in this passage is Alberti's insistence on the model being left unadorned and pure if it is to be used as a representational tool, since "the exhibition of models which have been coloured or which have been made attractive by painting clearly indicates that the architect does not seek simply to represent

his plan". In other words, the highly finished, colored, and decorated architectural model takes on a different meaning than a mere representational tool.

The model performs an important role in the architect's work in that it is the only representational technique that allows for a prefiguration of the finished building and thus for overall control of the form. Along with other representational techniques, it allows the architect to imagine the spaces that will be handled as the project evolves. Yet the model is perhaps the most ambiguous and the most misleading of all representational techniques precisely because it is an object. The only way in which a model can fulfill its role as an object representing space is by obviating its own purely representative function. That is to say, its form must maintain some measure of the incompleteness that is of the model's very nature. It now becomes clear that the models shown in this book are not architectural models, at least not in the original sense of the term. In fact the attention lavished on their manufacture, the precise rendering of each detail, and the exact reproduction of the materials to be used transform them into finished objects in their own right, with a life of their own. The model's link with architecture is in some sense broken here, for it no longer refers to something beyond itself, but takes on a final, finished meaning through its very existence. Instead of being an intermediate step toward the end result of a structure, the model becomes an end in itself.

Model of Procter & Gamble headquarters, Cincinnati, 1985, Kohn Pedersen Fox Associates. (Photo: Jock Pottle)

Above—Model of Atlantic Center, Atlanta, 1987, John Burgee Architects with Philip Johnson. (Photo: Hedrich Blessing)

Right—Model of The American Telephone & Telegraph Building, New York, 1985, Johnson/Burgee Associates. (Photo: Hedrich Blessing)

Model of The World Financial Center, New York, 1987, Cesar Pelli & Associates.
(Photo: Wolfgang Hoyt)

We are no longer dealing with models here, but with miniatures— objects that replace, rather than represent, architectural spaces. What then is their function, their meaning?

In order to reach an answer, we must first consider what a miniature is and above all the fascination it exerts on human beings. The seductive property of the miniature is certainly not due to its small size: do we allow ourselves to be seduced by pencil-sharpeners or buttons simply because they are small? What is fascinating about the miniature is that it reproduces with great precision and care a reality reduced in scale. In order to understand better, we could examine the sensations that certain toys evoked in us as children: are not toys often reproductions of people, spaces, and objects reduced in scale? Naturally, they are not as perfectly executed as miniatures, but children don't notice the difference; their eyes do not make as many demands as adult eyes, or at least they make different ones. For the child, reality is something confused and the toy reproduces its forms adequately.

What pleasure can a child draw from being surrounded by a world reduced in scale? In the first place, we have to remember that a reduction in scale of an object corresponds automatically to enlargement of the viewer. In other words, if the objects that surround us are reduced in scale, we feel bigger. Humans are subject to a powerful illusory mechanism: a reduction of scale in those objects we are used to seeing in a given dimension induces in us a feeling of superiority.

Since reality is on a scale of one-to-one, any alteration of this scale throws us into a fantastic, unreal dimension. Gulliver describes Lilliput as a country full of beauty, contrary to Brobdignag, whose deformed and disgusting aspects he continually emphasizes. The beauty of Lilliput corresponds to the pleasure of a man who considers himself to be a giant in the world, while the repugnant aspects of Brobdignag represent the unpleasant sensations produced by a world that incites fear and subjection, a world on a gigantic scale.

Thus the toy, in representing objects, spaces, and people on a reduced scale, introduces the child to a fantastic world in which the uncomfortable position of being small, dependent, and vulnerable is turned upside-down. In the fantastically real world of play, the child is able to satisfy a powerful desire—to be big, a desire that takes a long time to be satisfied in reality.

The miniature presents us with a similar reduction in scale, only here it is the adult and not the child who is to experience pleasure. For this reason, the miniature, unlike the toy, is characterized by the minuteness of its detail and the exactness of its reduction in scale: the adult, better acquainted with reality, apparently demands greater precision when its forms are reproduced.

But of what does the adult's pleasure consist? Something very similar to what is produced in the child by the toy. By making the forms that surround us smaller, those feelings of power and security that so often are thwarted by reality are reawakened. We are able

Detail of model of The World Financial
Center, New York, 1987, Cesar Pelli
& Associates. (Photo: Wolfgang Hoyt)

at last to satisfy our desire for dominion over the surrounding world,
for enlargement and reinforcement of our identities. The illusory
mechanism triggered by a reduction of scale reverses our perception
from one of a reality in which we are small, to one in which sud-
denly the smallness of everything around us makes us feel big, se-
cure, and dominant.

Thus it seems that the fundamental difference between an architectural model and a miniature lies in their relationships with reality.
The model brings us closer to reality by representing it, while the
miniature substitutes for reality some other dimension that has been
purified of reality's frightening and intimidating aspects.

We now can see that these objects, so accurately and ably executed,
actually manifest insecurity and fear of true architectonic space,
which in skyscrapers and big cities, it must be remembered, assumes
gigantic proportions. Fear of the external world is exorcised by reduc-

ing architectural space to an object. In this way the space, rather than possessing human life by containing it, materially speaking, becomes an object that can be possessed.

Main Street

Americans don't restrict themselves to miniaturizing skyscrapers—the whole world is miniaturized at Disney World. The tendency to beautify, to purify, to sweeten reality is nowhere so evident as in this amusement park.[3]

   At Disney World there is a reproduction of Main Street. In pioneer days, Main Street was the focal point of social life, providing entertainment, diversion, the opportunity to meet others. Its basic physical characteristic was a pleasing, friendly facade, a sort of pretty and carefree decor that had the power to make people forget for a moment the harshness of pioneer existence. The very sweetened-up version at Disney World greatly emphasizes this aspect. Disney World's Main Street cleans up and beautifies a place whose main characteristic was already to clean up and beautify reality. It is therefore the product of a double beautifying operation, a hyperbeautification. The beautification of the original Main Street was an attempt to mitigate the sufferings caused by a brutish reality. But to what need does this hyperbeautification respond? Our question obviously goes beyond the bounds of Disney World itself, although an amusement park is certainly the ideal place to set into motion this kind of mechanism. We refer as well to what Disney World has come to stand for in contemporary society.

Disney World's Main Street is not so much an idealization of the real thing as it is a filtering and package operation, involving the elimination of unpleasantness, of tragedy, of time and of blemish. But the real Main Street, the authentic nineteenth-century thing, is neither so facile nor so felicitous. It registers, instead, an optimistic desperation. The Greek temple, the false Victorian facade, the Palladian portico, the unused Opera-House, the courthouse sanctioned by the glamor of Napoleon III's Paris, the conspicuous monument to the Civil War or to the Fearless Fireman, these are the evidence of almost frenzied effort, via the movingly ingenious reconstruction of stable cultural images, to provide stability in an unstable scene, to convert frontier flux into established community. Main Street was never very pretty nor, probably, ever very prosperous; but it was a posture towards the world involving both independence and enterprise and it was never lacking in a rawness of pathetic dignity. Its clumsy, would-be metropolitan veneers are the indication of a certain stoicism of mood, of a sort of embittered flamboyance, which acquires its final dignity from its essential lack of success. That is, while Main Street was an often grand attempt to dissimulate real hardship and deprivation—an attempt which could only fail, one may still sometimes, even in its physical inadequacy, discern the implicit grandeur of its moral impulse.

Two views of Main Street at Disney World, Orlando, Fla. (Photos: Dida Biggi)

*In other words, the real Main Street, about which there may often
be something a little sardonic, is an exhibition of a reserved and scarcely
agreeable reality, of a reality which engages speculative curiosity, which
stimulates the imagination and which, for its understanding, insists on the
expenditure of mental energy. In the real Main Street there is, inevitably,
a two-way commerce between the observer and the observed; but the Disney
World version can scarcely allow for any such risky business. The Disney
World version cannot seriously emulate its enigmatic original. A machine
for the production of euphoria, it can only leave the imagination un-
provoked and the capacity for speculation unstimulated; and, while it
might be argued that the nausea produced by overexposure to sugar coating
and eternally fixed smiles might guarantee a certain genuine and unpleasant
emotional response, then there is surely some question (sado-masochism
notwithstanding) as to whether such a traumatic experience is really
necessary.[4]*

This is like saying that in particularly difficult situations a certain
idealization of reality can constitute a healthy defense mechanism,
while an excessive beautification (like all excesses) produces negative
results. It may guard us from trauma, but it also hampers maturation
and growth. This assumes particular importance in regard to a "society in its infancy," as American society undoubtedly is. Reality
might sometimes be very painful to look at, but there is no other way
for us to become adults instead of remaining as overgrown children.

NOTES

1. B. Zevi, *Saper Vedere L'Architettura* (Turin, Italy: Einaudi, 1948), 47.

2. L. B. Alberti, *De re Aedificatoria* (Milan: Ed. il Polifilo, 1966), 47.

3. Robert Venturi defines Disney World as "a symbolic American utopia,"
and further that "Disney World is nearer to what people really want
than what architects have ever given them." Quoted by Goldberger in
"Mickey Mouse Teaches the Architects," *The New York Times Magazine*,
22 October 1972. Copyright © 1972 by The New York Times Company.
Reprinted by permission.

4. C. Rowe, *Collage City* (Cambridge, MA: MIT Press, 1978), 46.

3

Beyond the Image

THE HEADQUARTERS SKYSCRAPER

The Headquarters Skyscraper: Its Image

There is an important difference between the commercial skyscraper and the headquarters skyscraper. While the commercial skyscraper houses the offices of a vast number of different firms, the headquarters skyscraper is the home office of one firm in particular.[1] A headquarters skyscraper sometimes also contains the offices of other firms, since the principal firm often leases or sells part of the excess space. The skyscraper's image and its name, however, remain the property of the firm it houses. Many American skyscrapers are headquarters buildings, especially the most important ones—AT&T, Citicorp, Pennzoil, and Seagram.

The image of the headquarters skyscraper has several burdens not shared by the commercial skyscraper: not only must it advertise the internal office space and increase its market value, it must also represent the face of the corporation whose head offices it houses. Although the headquarters may be a low building if it is situated outside an urban context, within the metropolis, in the form of a skyscraper, it can act as an extremely powerful advertising mechanism.[2] It will appear in newspapers and on postcards, in films and advertisements, and on television, becoming part of an almost endless advertising mechanism.

Because corporations have to do with the public, they must build up for themselves a prestige, a status and a reputation which will in some way work to the firm's advantage. This creation of images is directed primarily at clients, share-holders, competitors, executives and employees of the firm, and occasionally also at legislators, business critics, and writers. Architecture is just one of many means available to the heads of corporations for changing public opinion and improving public relations.[3]

Many of the corporation's problems stem from its fragmentation on the one hand and from its enormous dimensions on the other. To solve these problems the corporation needs an image that will somehow put everything back together, unify it, and make it, if not easily comprehensible, at least graspable. The architectural image allows the corporation to be "seen," to pass through the eyes into the minds of the public and the corporation's employees. To succeed, it is vitally important for it to reach both of these groups.

If the modern corporation intends to foster a favorable opinion of itself in society, it needs more than a "functional" image. If anything, it needs a strong visual image. Otherwise, it stands in constant danger of having no image at all. . . . The paramount role of the corporate headquarters continues to isolate the corporation's leadership from its tangible sources of power and wealth, the capital assets and personnel of its divisions, and these sources from each other. Thus, the identity of a corporation, its headquarters staff, divisions, products, and services, can be vague or even unknown to the public. A proliferation of abstract corporate names and logotypes and a growing tendency for products and services to become similar in nature regardless of their origin has only compounded the problem. Establishing a convincing identity for the contemporary corporate office facility is a challenge that should be taken for the sake of the corporation's own personnel if no one else's.[4]

The headquarters image therefore has three fundamental tasks: to publicize the corporation; to create favorable public opinion; and to offer employees an image with which to identify themselves.

This last point brings us to a more complex subject, since it implies going beyond the skyscraper's image and into what we may define as its "inside world." We shall limit ourselves to taking just a few steps inside the main door.

THE INSIDE WORLD

The Inside World of the Corporations

In very general and abstract terms (but then abstraction is characteristic of corporations and is why they depend on architecture to give

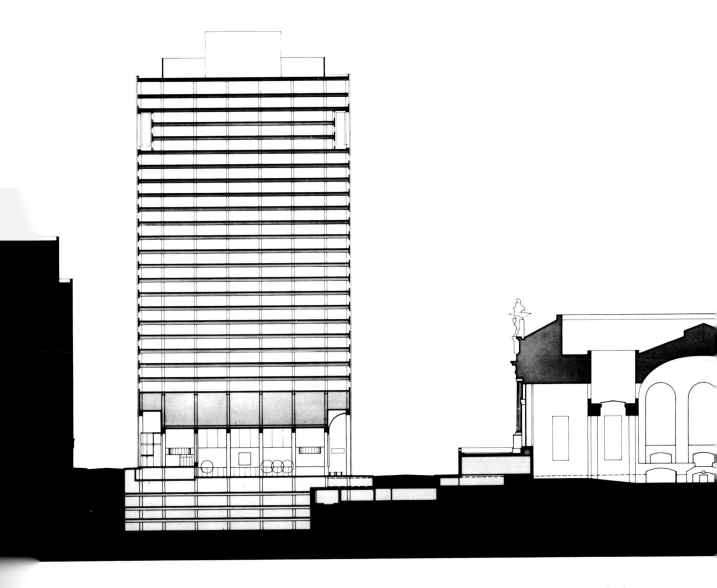

Philip Morris headquarters: North-South section, New York, 1984, Ulrich Franzen & Associates Architects.

concreteness), the corporation is a sort of "society" unto itself, its own "laws," "values," and "culture."[5] In order for employees as productive as possible, they must, to a certain extent, iden- with the corporation. Obviously the headquarters image alone is nough to establish the identification of the employee with the it is only one of the many techniques used by managers to this

the introduction to *In Search of Excellence* we find the following ge:

The psychologist Ernest Becker . . . has staked out a major supporting theoretical position, albeit one ignored by most management analysts. He argues that man is driven by an essential "dualism"; he needs both to be a part of something and to stick out. He needs at one and the same time to be a conforming member of a winning team and to be a star in his own right. . . . The best-managed companies, and a few others, act in accordance with these theories. For example, the manager of a 100-person sales branch rented the Meadowlands Stadium (New Jersey) for the evening. After work, his salesmen ran onto the stadium's field through the player's tunnel. As each emerged, the electronic scoreboard beamed his name to the assembled crowd. Executives from corporate headquarters, employees from other offices, and family and friends were present, cheering loudly. The company is IBM. With one act (most nonexcellent companies would write it off as too corny, too lavish, or both), IBM simultaneously reaffirmed its heroic dimension (satisfying the individual's need to be a part of something great) and its concern for individual self-expression (the need to stick out). IBM is bridging an apparent paradox. If there is one striking feature of the excellent companies, it is this ability to manage ambiguity and paradox. What our rational economist friends tell us ought not to be possible the excellent companies do routinely.[6]

It is important to know this in order to understand, if only vaguely, the internal workings of multinationals. One of the basic ingredients for their success is their ability to count on so-called exemplary workers. In other words, a highly intensive pace of work is expected of their employees. And in order to obtain this, a very particular environment is created. The methods used are not openly coercive; they work at a subconscious level, through the environment. The success of corporations depends to a great extent on the pressures exercised on the irrational dimension of human beings—human beings defined solely as either client or employee.

Despite the inappropriateness of the terms—given that millions of people live and work in headquarters skyscrapers—we might define this type of skyscraper as a sort of gigantic machine that transmits and stimulates. It transmits by sending out powerful advertising messages and stimulates by working internally to increase employee productivity. This is why it is amazing to so often find the skyscraper discussed solely in terms relating to visual image. Never has so much attention been paid to the form, the appearance, of a machine. One might have expected a description of the mechanisms of such a refined machine as this.

Corporation as Machine

The corporation may also be thought of as a machine with gears made up of the people who work for it. In the same way that efficient-working gears require oil (to use mechanical terms that are almost prehistoric by now), an environment must be created for employees that will allow them to act quickly and precisely, to be organized and productive. It is therefore a question of discovering which factors influence people to behave in the most efficient way. The answers are supplied by sociologists, anthropologists, and students of human behavior working in various universities or private institutions. On this basis, the work environment, and more generally the external environment, is then created.

The W. C. Decker Engineering Building project is an important example of this. Seven hundred and forty engineers work inside this building. It was built by Corning Glass Works Co., with the aim of increasing their workers' productivity by 15 percent.

Corning executives wanted to make the Decker center "a significant statement about our commitment to engineering and productivity," in the words of James R. Houghton, vice chairman and strategic officer . . . Toward this end, Corning turned to Dr. Thomas J. Allen, professor of organizational psychology and management at MIT's Sloan School of Management, to find how engineers work. Corning also commissioned the New York firm of Davis, Brody & Associates for architecture and interior design . . . Corning wanted to house 740 engineers and support personnel in an environment free of those obstacles that would short-circuit creative interaction and thus productivity. . . . In charge of the project, David E. Leibson, then senior vice president and director of the Manufacturing and Engineering Division, says: "Our primary goal was a 15 percent increase in productivity—that is, an increase in new projects while keeping employment level." Instrumental in bringing this goal to reality was the working relationship of the Davis, Brody architects and Dr. Allen. During the past 15 years, Dr. Allen (author of Managing the Flow of Technology *published by MIT Press) had studied the work patterns of researchers and scientists. Communication, he concludes, is the key to productivity. Dr. Allen's finding showed that more than 80 percent of an engineer's ideas come from face-to-face contact with colleagues. They dislike using the phone, will not walk more than 100 feet to discuss an idea or gather information, and avoid using elevators. "Distance," Dr. Allen says, "decays interaction." Davis, Brody deftly translated Dr. Allen's findings into a three-story structure that has optimum visibility of every floor, strategically placed ramps, stairs and escalators to encourage vertical movement, and an open plan layout and informal gathering places for maximum communication—all within a fully flexible framework.[7]*

Other companies have joined Corning in trying to boost productivity through improved employee communication.

Another vital spur to informal communication is the deployment of simple physical configurations. Corning Glass installed escalators (rather than elevators) in its new engineering building to increase the chance of face-to-face contact. 3M sponsors clubs for many groups of a dozen or so employees for the sole purpose of increasing the probability of stray problem-

solving sessions at lunch time and in general. A Citibank officer noted that in one department the age-old operations–versus–lending-officer split was solved when everybody in the group moved to the same floor with their desks intermingled. What does it all add up to? Lots of communication.[8]

Space and Behavior

In *Science and Human Behavior*, B. F. Skinner writes that people are to a great extent the product of the stimuli they receive from the external world, and that if the environment is defined with sufficient precision, the actions of the individual can be accurately predicted. It is therefore possible, Skinner affirms, to direct people toward predetermined behavior patterns by adjusting the environment surrounding them.[9] This type of manipulation of the human will through the external environment does not involve the use of force, nor of authoritarian or punitive methods, since it remains confined to an irrational dimension. Human beings, in other words, are not aware of being subjected to strong external influences, because their relationships with their environment are for the most part unconscious.

It should be understood that by environment we mean human relationships and space. We will focus our attention on the latter.

Skinner's theories, like those of other students of human behavior, are applied most often in the workplace and the market place: in offices, shops, supermarkets, and large department stores, and also in fast food outlets. But it is in corporate headquarters that these manipulative techniques of influencing human behavior by means of the environment become particularly evident.

Roughly speaking, the headquarters of a corporation is an assembly of carefully planned spaces whose form has been defined according to the amount of work expected of the employees. It is a space planned on the basis of the results of research conducted for many years at major universities, including M.I.T., Stanford, and Harvard. Naturally, this research is financed by the corporations.[10]

In *Corporate Design*, a book that examines the interiors of headquarters built in America in recent years, the authors show how important it is to introduce plants, colors, smells, and rough and soft materials, since employee productivity levels can be increased by stimulating all the senses. As further evidence for their theory, they point to E. T. Hall's finding in *The Hidden Dimension* that human beings explore their environment by using all their senses and that such experience is directly linked to their actions.[11]

It is not true to say that *all* senses are stimulated in the new corporate skyscraper, though we can certainly say that they are more stimulating spaces than those built in the 1950s. *Complete* sensory stimulation probably would not have the desired effect on productivity.

Facing page—Best Products headquarters: general offices, Richmond, Va., 1981, Hardy, Holzman, Pfeiffer Architects. (Photo © 1981 Norman McGrath, ASMP)

In *The Hidden Dimension* Hall states, in fact, that cultures with the most lively sensory perceptions (he cites Arabs as an example) tend not to feature great levels of productivity.

What is involved in the corporate skyscraper is a purely nervous kind of stimulation, despite the presence of plants, waterfalls, and the like. It creates excitement, it does not invite languid abandon or poetic transport, nor does it intend to.

Corporate interiors are subdivided according to function and according to a precise hierarchy. The staff of a corporation may be roughly divided into two groups: executives and employees (although this division is imprecise because it omits middle management and support staff). Each of these groups is allotted its own space. The employees work in the typical office floors: open-plan spaces with conference rooms, kitchens, cafeterias, toilets, recreation spaces, and so on. Unlike the executives, clerical staff members have no right to privacy, and they must work in spaces where continual contact with others is unavoidable. Walls, partitions, and closed offices are the privileges of managers.

Facing page, top—Philip Morris headquarters: corridors, New York, 1984, Ulrich Franzen & Associates Architects. (Photo © 1984 Norman McGrath, ASMP)

Facing page, bottom—Philip Morris headquarters: cafeteria, New York, 1984, Ulrich Franzen & Associates Architects. (Photo © 1984 Norman McGrath, ASMP)

Below—Scor Reinsurance headquarters: general offices, Dallas, 1984, PLM Design, Inc. (Photo: Mark Ross)

An executive office suite available from Stow & Davis. (Courtesy Steelcase Inc.)

General Offices

The open-plan design used on typical office floors is suited to the highly mobile nature of general office activity. It makes for a flexible, adaptable space that can be rapidly extended or restricted according to necessity. The use of panels and work stations allows continual modification of its form.

The typical office floor is a transparent space, visible as a whole and easily navigated; essentially, it is one single enormous office devoid of barriers to vision or locomotion. The spaces are not divided by walls or partitions but by moveable, screenlike panels that allow employees the minimum visual and acoustic privacy necessary to work. In addition, the space must stimulate and encourage interaction among staff.

The sight of one's colleagues hard at work is an incitement to work oneself, while the constant movement and the frenetic activity of the office predisposes employees to work, gets them involved, excites their nervous systems. By allowing employees to look at each other,

Office workers, as shown in a Herman Miller advertisement. (Courtesy of Herman Miller, Inc.)

U.S. Trust Corporation: general offices, 770 Broadway, New York, 1981, Haines Lundberg Waehler. (Photos © 1981 Norman McGrath, ASMP)

meet, and talk, the space stimulates them to want to do so. In this
sense, space structures human relationships. It should be pointed out
that the distinction made here between space and human relationships is useful but not very correct, in that the two are very closely
connected in forming the external environment.

The midheight panels of work stations allow an overall view of
the larger space and, at the same time, give the employees their own
territory. Permitting the employees to furnish their own desk tops
with personal objects creates security, in that it permits the exercise
of some small measure of power. Although small, this gesture seems
nonetheless to be capable of setting off an illusionary mechanism
that makes the employees believe they possess more power than they
actually have. Psychologists in a field called "illusion of control"
study this unique human mechanism.[12] It is a way of protecting
employees from mental situations (such as awareness of their aliena-
tion) that would have a negative effect on productivity.

AT&T Long Lines Eastern Regional Headquarters: general offices, Oakton, Va.,
1980, dePolo/Dunbar Inc. Interior Designers and Kohn Pedersen Fox Associates
Architects. (Photo: Ezra Stoller © Esto)

In the wide-open spaces created by the open plan, work stations create corners of privacy, important not only from a functional point of view, but also psychologically.

Most corporations today are using open plan systems in their general office areas. But before going to any new plan, a company should consider how much visual and acoustic privacy is desirable for each employee. If needs vary, then perhaps the work situations should vary as well.

The problem is how to give each individual a sense of his own dignity and uniqueness when everyone is being treated as equals. One solution is to offer choice whenever possible and to allow employees to personalize their work stations. The results may not be to the designer's liking, but people need to feel they have control over their own workplace before they can truly identify with the company.[13]

In corporate headquarters, functional needs continually overlap with psychological ones.

U.S. News and World Report: work station, Washington, 1984, Deupi and Associates. (Photo © Maxwell MacKenzie)

International Paper headquarters: general offices, New York, 1983, The Space
Design Group. (Photo: Mark Ross)

Chemical Bank: general offices, New York, 1982, Haines Lundberg Waehler.
(Photo: James D'Addio)

Philip Morris headquarters: cafeteria, New York, 1984, Ulrich Franzen & Associates Architects. (Photo © 1984 Norman McGrath, ASMP)

National Westminster Bank USA: cafeteria, New York, 1984, The Space Design
Group. (Photo: Mark Ross)

AT&T Long Lines Eastern Regional Headquarters: general offices, Oakton, Va., 1980, dePolo/Dunbar Inc. Interior Designers and Kohn Pedersen Fox Associates Architects. (Photo: Ezra Stoller © Esto)

Cafeterias and Dining Rooms

The purpose of the corporate cafeteria is not only to avoid wasted time but also to reinforce the process of cohesion among employees. It is an environment that should relax people (behavior can be more informal here than in the office) and at the same time stimulate them—through colors, light effects, plants, paintings, or fountains—so that employees will return to work recharged.

The hierarchical distinctions that mark corporate headquarters are maintained in the spaces reserved for lunch. Executives have their own eating area, usually small, with a few simply yet luxuriously laid tables. Unlike the cafeterias, these executive dining rooms have an important practical function, since they will host numerous business lunches. Expensive fabrics, fine woods, and silverware are present, to show that to eat here is a true privilege, and that whoever is invited here is almost part of the "family." These areas owe their existence to the knowledge that moments of pleasure and distraction are useful means of increasing productivity.

Philip Morris headquarters: plan of the ground floor, New York, 1984, Ulrich Franzen & Associates Architects.

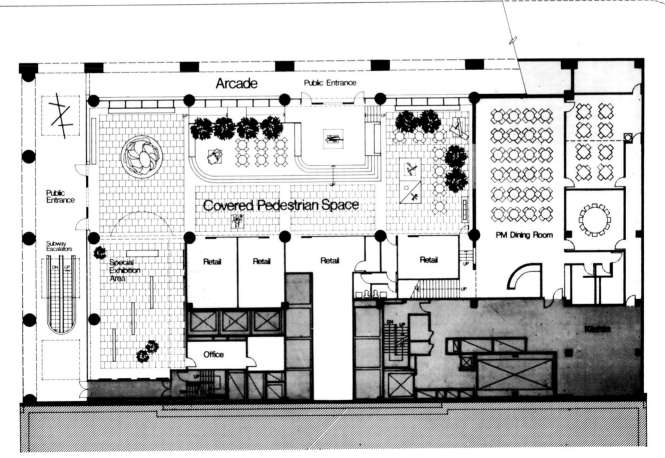

PARK AVENUE

E. 42nd STREET

Arcade

Public Entrance

Public Entrance

Covered Pedestrian Space

Subway Escalators

Special Exhibition Area

Retail   Retail   Retail   Retail

Office

PM Dining Room

Kitchen

Right—U.S. News and World Report: cafeteria, Washington, 1984, Deupi and Associates. (Photo © Maxwell MacKenzie)

U.S. Trust Corporation: cafeteria, New York, 1981, Haines Lundberg Waehler. (Photo © 1981 Norman McGrath, ASMP)

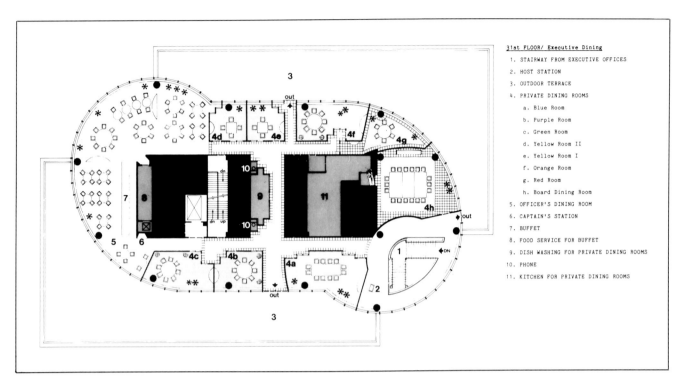

31st FLOOR/ Executive Dining

1. STAIRWAY FROM EXECUTIVE OFFICES
2. HOST STATION
3. OUTDOOR TERRACE
4. PRIVATE DINING ROOMS
   a. Blue Room
   b. Purple Room
   c. Green Room
   d. Yellow Room II
   e. Yellow Room I
   f. Orange Room
   g. Red Room
   h. Board Dining Room
5. OFFICER'S DINING ROOM
6. CAPTAIN'S STATION
7. BUFFET
8. FOOD SERVICE FOR BUFFET
9. DISH WASHING FOR PRIVATE DINING ROOMS
10. PHONE
11. KITCHEN FOR PRIVATE DINING ROOMS

National Westminster Bank USA: plan of the 31st floor, where the executive dining rooms are located, New York, 1984, The Space Design Group. (Photo: Mark Ross)

National Westminster Bank USA: executive dining floor details, New York, 1984, The Space Design Group. **Left**—a private dining room. **Right**—a table set for lunch. (Photos: Mark Ross)

National Westminster Bank USA: executive dining floor details, New York, 1984, The Space Design Group. **Facing page, clockwise from upper left** — corridor; flooring detail; serving counter in officers' dining room; undulating wall in the Board's dining room. **This page, clockwise from upper left** — upper wall details; the Yellow Room set for lunch; view of entry corridor from the stairwell. (Photos: Mark Ross)

Reliance Group Holdings offices:
cafeteria, New York, 1979, Gwathmey
Siegel & Associates Architects. (Photo:
Jaime Ardiles-Arce)

Circulation

Circulation within the building is organized to allow for swift and easy access but also so that employees' spirits are recharged as they move about. The effects created by lights, juxtaposition of forms and materials, undulating wall surfaces, and works of art all work to stimulate the employee who gets up from the desk and heads to a meeting, goes for coffee, or seeks out a colleague to discuss a problem.

Those spaces destined as throughways are neutral areas whose task is to separate different functions. Because they are a sort of no-man's land, the person passing through them experiences a greater freedom to express his or her own thoughts. The armchairs positioned here and there along these throughways invite employees to stop and talk. Bosses aim strategically to foster these encounters because they strengthen the feeling of cohesion among company employees and because, by encouraging casual brainstorming, these improvised encounters can turn into valuable work sessions.

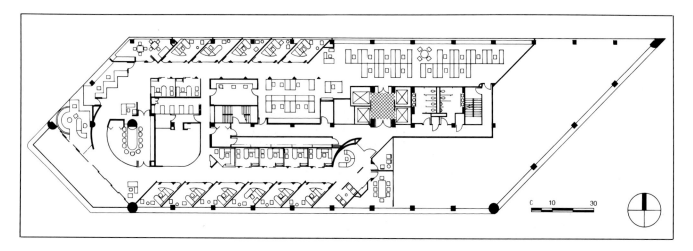

Floor plan of Wilshire Associates, Santa Monica, 1981, Gensler and Associates/ Architects.

U.S. Trust Corporation: reception area, New York, 1981, Haines Lundberg
Waehler. (Photo © 1981 Norman McGrath, ASMP)

Scor Reinsurance headquarters: reception area, Dallas, 1984, PLM Design, Inc.
(Photo: Mark Ross)

Above—National Westminster Bank USA: corridor through service area, New York, 1984, The Space Design Group. (Photo: Mark Ross)

International Paper headquarters: reception area, Purchase, N.Y. 1988, The Space Design Group. (Photo: Mark Ross)

International Paper headquarters:
corridor, Purchase, N.Y., 1988, The
Space Design Group. (Photo: Mark Ross)

Scor Reinsurance headquarters: detail of stairs, Dallas, 1984, PLM Design, Inc. (Photo: Mark Ross)

Best Products headquarters: corridor and stairs, Richmond, Va., 1981, Hardy, Holzman, Pfeiffer Architects. (Photo © 1981, Norman McGrath, ASMP)

Facing page—International Paper headquarters: waiting area, New York, 1983, The Space Design Group. (Photo: Mark Ross)

International Paper headquarters: two corridor views, Purchase, N.Y., 1988, The Space Design Group. (Photos: Mark Ross)

Hercules Inc. headquarters: atrium corridor, Wilmington, Del., 1983, Kohn
Pedersen Fox Associates. (Photo © 1983 Norman McGrath, ASMP)

McDonnell Douglas Automation Center: escalators, Dallas, 1984, Hellmuth,
Obata & Hassabaum, Inc. (Photo: George Silk)

Above—Philip Morris headquarters: entrance to cafeteria, New York, 1984, Ulrich Franzen & Associates Architects. (Photo © 1984 Norman McGrath, ASMP)

Right—Reliance Group Holdings offices: corridor, New York, 1979, Gwathmey Siegel & Associates Architects. (Photo: Jaime Ardiles-Arce)

Conference Rooms

It is in conference rooms, and particularly in the boardroom, that the corporation's strategy is determined, contracts negotiated, agreements reached, reports read, and so forth. Conference tables, from the small round extension that appears at the side of the work station to the table used in the boardroom, also have the fundamental task of helping to knit together, unite, amalgamate a highly specialized and consequently fragmented work staff. They crop up continually (and symptomatically) in headquarters buildings, in different forms— round, oval, rectangular, horseshoe-shaped—and different dimensions. In the conference rooms, too, although in a different way from other headquarters environments, the external environment makes up for a lack in the internal world. In fact, it is not just in the room but around the meeting table itself that the process of synthesis takes place.

These spaces are not planned by the architect: the architect simply translates into space the requirements that have been set by the corporation. The way in which the space is to be organized is decided by the corporation managers and the human behavior researchers.

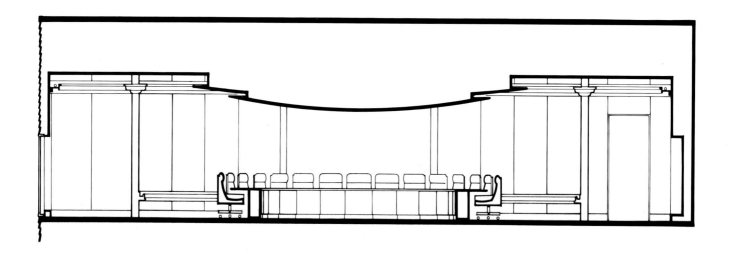

Plan of General Foods corporate headquarters: section of conference room, Rye, N.Y., 1977, Kevin Roche John Dinkeloo and Associates.

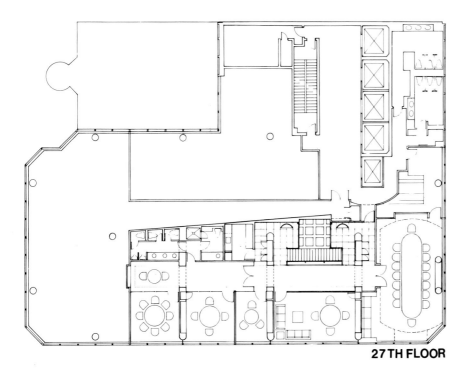

27 TH FLOOR

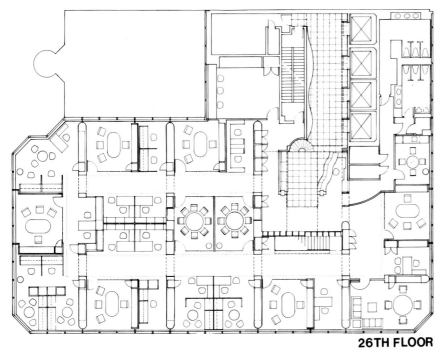

26TH FLOOR

Alusuisse of America offices: two floor plans, New York, 1983, Samuel J. DeSanto and Associates.

Reliance Group Holdings offices: detail of conference table and wall, New York, 1979, Gwathmey Siegel & Associates Architects. (Photo: Jaime Ardiles-Arce)

126

Above—Philip Morris headquarters: boardroom, New York, 1984, Ulrich Franzen & Associates Architects. (Photo © 1984 Norman McGrath, ASMP)

AT&T Long Lines Eastern Regional Headquarters: executive conference area, Oakton, Va., 1980, dePolo/Dunbar Inc. Interior Designers and Kohn Pedersen Fox Associates Architects. (Photo: Ezra Stoller © Esto)

The First Gibraltar Building: conference room, Houston, 1983, Morris Architects (formerly Morris/Aubry Architects). (Photo: Chas McGrath)

BBDO: "Midway" conference room, New York, 1987, The Space Design Group.
(Photo: Mark Ross)

International Paper headquarters: boardroom, Purchase, N.Y. 1988, The Space Design Group. (Photo: Mark Ross)

Reliance Group Holdings offices: conference room, New York, 1979, Gwathmey Siegel & Associates Architects. (Photo: Jaime Ardiles-Arce)

The Atrium

Usually situated just inside the main entrance of the building, the atrium is a large space, several floors high. Furnished with ramps, stairs, escalators, and elevators, it gives the impression of kinetic activity, of people coming in and out of offices, going up and down stairs, stopping in coffee lounges. The aim of the atrium is to infuse the employee with a sense of unity, to promote a sense of belonging to a whole, and therefore identifying with it.

The atrium may also be found at the center of a headquarters building where it forms the pivot around which the space of the whole building is arranged. This is usually the case when general headquarters are located outside of urban contexts. It may also occupy any number of other points in the available space. But the only way of telling that it is not in the center is by looking at the building's plans—entering the atrium, one at least has the sensation of being in a central and collective space. The employee must internalize and carry about this sensation.

Below and facing page—Reliance Group Holdings offices: three floor plans, New York, 1979, Gwathmey Siegel & Associates Architects.

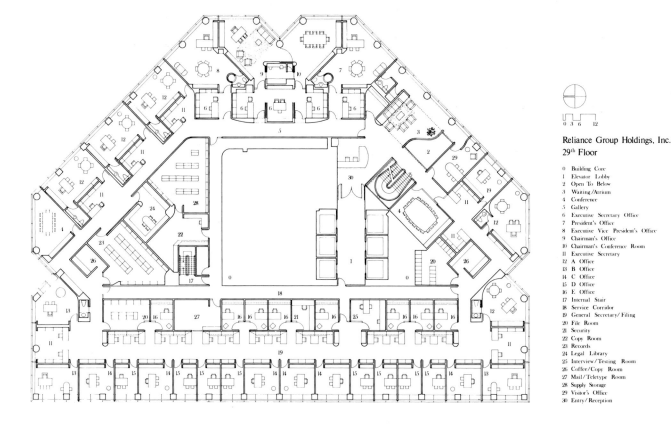

0 3 6   12

**Reliance Group Holdings, Inc.
29th Floor**

0   Building Core
1   Elevator Lobby
2   Open To Below
3   Waiting/Atrium
4   Conference
5   Gallery
6   Executive Secretary Office
7   President's Office
8   Executive Vice President's Office
9   Chairman's Office
10 Chairman's Conference Room
11 Executive Secretary
12 A Office
13 B Office
14 C Office
15 D Office
16 E Office
17 Internal Stair
18 Service Corridor
19 General Secretary/Filing
20 File Room
21 Security
22 Copy Room
23 Records
24 Legal Library
25 Interview/Testing Room
26 Coffee/Copy Room
27 Mail/Teletype Room
28 Supply Storage
29 Visitor's Office
30 Entry/Reception

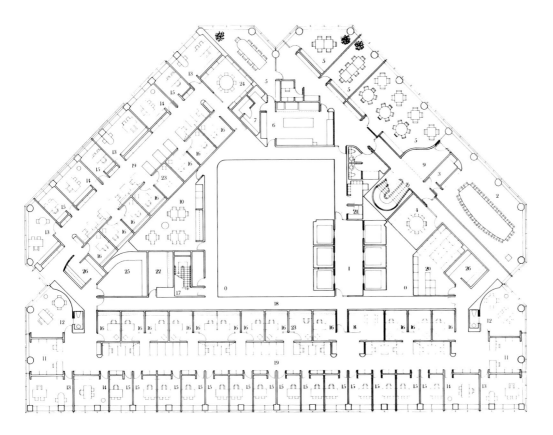

Reliance Group Holdings, Inc.
28th Floor

0 Building Core
1 Elevator Lobby
2 Board Room
3 Projection
4 Conference
5 Dining Room
6 Kitchen
7 Kitchen Storage
8 Audit
9 Atrium
10 Employee Lunchroom
11 Executive Secretary
12 A Office
13 B Office
14 C Office
15 D Office
16 E Office
17 Internal Stair
18 Service Corridor
19 General Secretary / Filing
20 File Room
21 Security
22 Copy Room
23 Computer Terminal
24 Library
25 Word Processing
26 Coffee / Copy Room

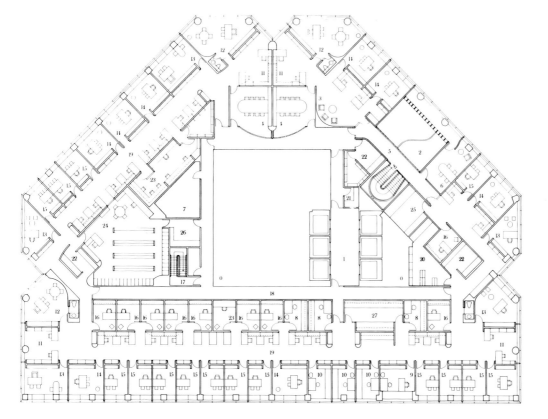

Reliance Group Holdings, Inc.
30th Floor

0 Building Core
1 Elevator Lobby
2 Open To Below
3 Waiting Room
4 Conference
5 Balcony
6 Visitor's Office
7 Telephone Equipment
8 Architect
9 Chief Architect
10 Architect
11 Executive Secretary
12 A Office
13 B Office
14 C Office
15 D Office
16 E Office
17 Internal Stair
18 Service Corridor
19 General Secretary / Filing
20 File Room
21 Security
22 Coffee / Copy Room
23 Computer Terminal
24 Library
25 Computer Terminal / Flat File
26 Copy Room
27 Blueprint / Flat File

Republic Bank Center: atrium, Houston, 1984, Johnson/Burgee Architects. (Photo: Richard Payne)

The atrium is the entrance, the town square, the place of brief meetings and visual stimulation. One feels oneself exposed, and everybody else is too. The bosses' gaze is also present, if not directly visible—they observe, often from inside glass-walled offices.

Here, as in the general offices, the space does not interfere with but rather encourages meetings and exchanges between staff. Yet it is not a space that encourages human relationships—only one particular kind of human relationship. True, deep human relationships must be considered distractions as far as executives' goals are concerned. The only aspects of human relationships accorded any importance are those that stimulate the desire to get ahead, to stand out, to win. Among the types of relationships that can be established between individuals, it is the competitive one that is most encouraged, since it creates tension and nervous excitement, and is full of a powerful (and painful) energy that is perfect for applying toward work.[14]

The atrium and open-plan offices encourage high levels of activity and movement (a space that permits movement in turn leads people to move). The value of a space accrues from what one can do in it and how one sees it. One is active because one *can* be so and because activity is obsessively perceived.

Space facilitates movement and action, it structures human relationships, and renders perceptible the presence of others, their movements, and their frenetic activity.

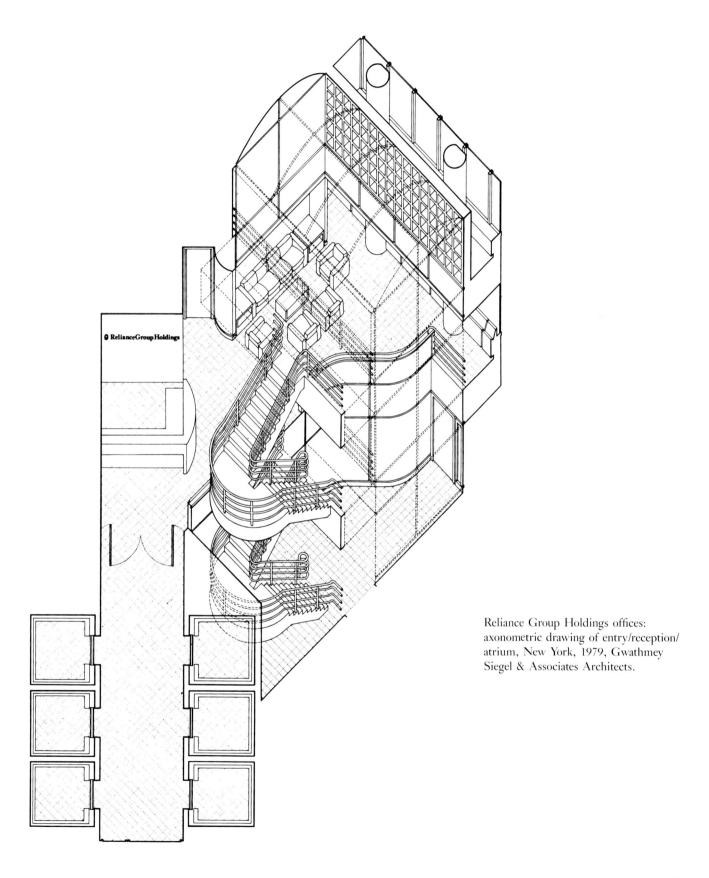

Reliance Group Holdings offices:
axonometric drawing of entry/reception/
atrium, New York, 1979, Gwathmey
Siegel & Associates Architects.

Philip Morris headquarters: atrium, New York, 1984, Ulrich Franzen & Associates Architects.

Facing Page—Corporate headquarters/ Research and Development facility, Hollister, Inc., Libertyville, Il., 1981, Holabird & Root Architects. (Photo © 1981 Howard N. Kaplan/HNK Architectural Photography, Inc.)

In the interior of a building, large open spaces like galerias and atriums which penetrate for several floors facilitate visual contacts and casual encounters among employees. This kind of openness not only improves communication, but also fosters a sense of community—the feeling that employees are part of a family. Creativity and individuality are encouraged by such an environment and this, in turn, promotes technical skill, job performance and a sense of personal well-being which ultimately translates into greater profits for the corporation.[15]

Several aspects of the relationships established within the corporate headquarters recall those in the family. The authoritative position of the manager shares a number of characteristics with the father figure. The employees, subject to the enormous pressure exercised by feelings of competition, find themselves similar to brothers and sisters competing for the love of their parents. The main differences lie in the intensity and depth of these feelings and in their aims. Family feelings are considerably deformed in the corporation. Yet something remains: some studies show that, on leaving a corporation, many ex-employees have serious difficulty readapting to the outside world.[16]

The corporations' use of feelings that are developed within the family context is also evidenced in the general structure of the headquarters' space. The inside of a headquarters resembles a large house, with some rooms reserved for the adults (managers), open spaces reserved for the children (employees), dining rooms, kitchens, toilets, and meeting rooms. The bosses and the employees of a corporation in these ways echo the figures of parents and children.

Above—Republic Bank Center: atrium, Houston, 1984, Johnson/Burgee Architects. (Photo: Richard Payne)

Right—Pennzoil Place: atrium, Houston, 1976, Johnson/Burgee Architects. (Photo: Richard Payne)

Above—Northwestern Terminal: entrance to atrium, Chicago, 1985,
Murphy/Jahn Architects. (Photo: Murphy/Jahn Architects)

Left—AT&T Long Lines Eastern Regional Headquarters: atrium, Oakton, Va.,
1980, dePolo/Dunbar Inc. Interior Designers and Kohn Pedersen Fox Associates
Architects. (Photo: Ezra Stoller © Esto)

Executive Offices

The executives' area is a distinct area of the headquarters. It is the only part that is isolated and enclosed by walls. It is the part with the most representative function, in that it must reflect the general image of the corporation. It has features that are markedly similar to those of an apartment; it could even be said that it is very lavishly furnished in the manner of a luxury apartment.

The space is divided up into a series of enclosed environments, each with its specific function: reception, dining rooms, kitchens, toilets.

The waiting rooms resemble large living rooms while the dining rooms are designed in such a way as to create an intimate, family atmosphere for working lunches. In the boardroom, meetings are held to decide on strategy, negotiate contracts, and reach agreements.

If the clerical workers' space is interesting because of how it has been designed to create the maximum stimuli, that of the executives is interesting because of its theatrical character. From the carpets to the chairs, tables, and paintings hanging on the walls, everything is calculated as if it formed a stage set in a theater. Everything in this area must visibly express and reflect power. To this end, luxury is a good means of communication.

In the executive office, the furniture and the objects and their arrangement are decided on according to the effects they are intended to produce. The more distant the desk from the door, the deeper and taller the backrest of the armchair in which the executive sits, the more powerful he will appear. Space acts like a powerful amplifier for increasing and emphasizing the power of the executive. The importance of anthropological and ethological studies in the planning of such spaces now becomes evident. The concept of territoriality, which comes from studies of animal behavior, is here used to establish the distances that are to be created by the arrangement of the furniture. The relationship between the executive's chair and the visitor's is determined by distances that researchers have categorized as intimate, private, social, and public. Some social distance (from 7 to 12 feet) is helpful to the executive in the exercise of power.[17]

The furnishing of the executive's office is more or less codified: on one side, an executive-sized desk; on the other, the conversation corner, complete with sofa, armchairs, and coffee table, as well as valuable ornaments. Along with or instead of the conversation corner, there might be a conference table.

Compared with the desk, the conversation corner offers more intimacy: social distance is reduced to the private level (from 4 to 7 feet). Whether the executive directs his guest to the desk or to the conversation corner determines the tone of an encounter.

In offices such as these the guest is at an obvious disadvantage. Every element of the setting reinforces the executive's power and at the same time weakens that of his interlocutors. Certain contri-

National Westminster Bank USA: reception area, New York, 1984, The Space
Design Group. (Photo: Mark Ross)

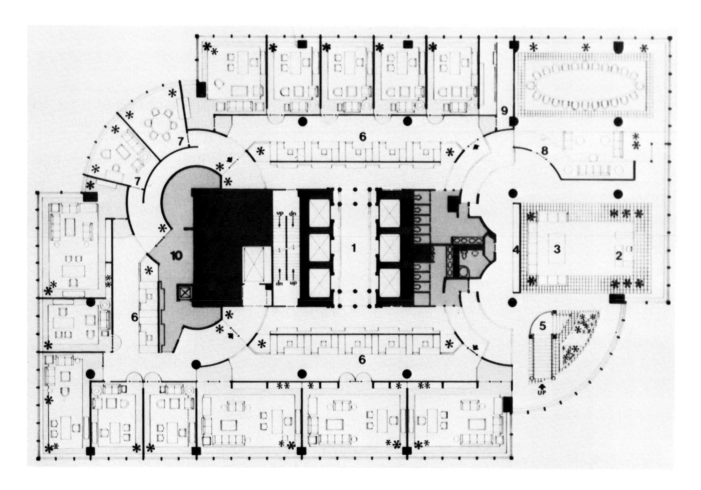

National Westminster Bank USA: floor plan of executive offices, New York, 1984,
The Space Design Group. (Photo: Mark Ross)

vances are used to this end. For example, some executives choose for themselves large, comfortable armchairs, leaving their guests to sit in low and particularly uncomfortable seats. This is just one way of forcing one's adversary into a physically and psychologically uncomfortable situation.[18]

Executive office furniture also serves to gratify and reassure the executive. The frequent use of antique reproductions is owed to their capacity to communicate solidity and security. The environment is used to offset on a formal level (and therefore on the level of illusion) some of the more unpleasant and above all harmful sensations produced by reality. Antique styles are used to create feelings of solidity and tranquillity that seem altogether lacking in reality. The potential of space to influence human senses is used to influence certain human responses, to stimulate and/or anesthetize certain feelings, according the executive's needs.

From all this we may deduce that (1) a space that stimulates activity is a space that first of all *permits* activity, because space is perceived according to the possible activity it can contain; (2) most of the relationships that humans establish with space are unconscious. We feel positive or negative, oppressed or stimulated, without knowing exactly what it is that produces these feelings; (3) space may provoke an infinite number of sensations and reactions over a wide range of gradations, from barely perceptible to very strong.

This last point may well contain the basic problem of corporate interior space: the amount of nervous stimulation that it produces. While it is true to say that space permits movement, it must also be said that it obliges movement. While space stimulates human creativity, it must be added that it forces humans to produce.

It is all very well to say that a work space must allow people to move about and to establish contact with others. The physical barriers (walls) that impede movement and a view of the whole may be perceived as obstacles and impediments; they may be accepted as limits. There are certainly situations in which these barriers are necessary: when there is need for intimacy, isolation, concentration, or attention. In this sense, external space is felt to be an extension of internal space (note that this latter spatial organization is reserved for high-ranking executives).

Yet these spaces are not only open—they are spaces in which openness and transparency are obsessively emphasized. And this is the point at which the limits are crossed. More than stimuli, they make us think of coercion applied on an unconscious level. It implies that human beings are empty vessels and, like machines, need an electric current to make them work.

Facing page—National Westminster Bank, USA: **above**—President's office; **below**—Chairman's office, New York, 1984, The Space Design Group. (Photos: Mark Ross)

Best Products headquarters: executive office, Richmond, Va., 1981, Hardy, Holzman, Pfeiffer Architects. (Photo © 1981 Norman McGrath, ASMP)

Evans Partnership offices: executive office, Parsippany, N.J., 1977, Gwathmey
Siegel & Associates Architects. (Photo: Jaime Ardiles-Arce)

Above—Scor Reinsurance headquarters: executive office, Dallas, 1984, PLM Design, Inc. (Photo: Mark Ross)

Left (above and below)—LTV corporate headquarters: executive offices, Dallas, 1985, PLM Design, Inc. (Photos: Mark Ross)

The Think Tank

The psychological tenet on which the McDonald's Think Tank is founded holds that there are two types of mental activity: one concentrates all its energy on the problem to be resolved; the other arrives at the solution by abandoning itself to free association. It is the latter mental attitude that is the more creative.

The central offices of McDonald's Co. contain a small room that has the specific function of stimulating creativity. It is a very special sort of space: nothing about it resembles the work environment or the rest of the building—nor any other space on earth. It is an atmosphere that takes one into another dimension: directly inside the human head. People who come in can lose themselves on a big cushion in the form of a brain.

In order to enter this Think Tank, one has to pass through a sort of labyrinth that functions to disconnect any links with the office environment. Additional features reinforce the feeling of detachment:

The executive enters from the entry passageway. He ascends three steps—to indicate another change in environment—removes his shoes, and passes through the hatch. The room is restful. The floor is really an upholstered, 8-foot, circular 700-gallon waterbed heated to 72 degrees fahrenheit. The executive can sit or lie there with no vertical or solid horizontal reference points to catch his eye. With the door closed, the room becomes a padded capsule with walls inclined 45 degrees to meet the domed ceiling. Every element of this environment is under the executive's control. He can adjust the lighting, and in this way lose the ceiling plane completely if he chooses. He can even hook up a machine called an alpha pacer that will beep when he generates alpha waves, an indication that he's becoming detached from his work environment and beginning to free-associate.[19]

NOTES

1. Large corporations own numerous isolated offices and several regional offices as well as a world headquarters. By bringing general and executive offices under one roof, these regional or world headquarters allow us to analyze certain aspects of the office environment that remain invisible in isolated offices. These are ideal conditions in which to see that those characteristics that stand out most obviously in the corporate headquarters are also present in smaller offices.

2. Regional headquarters are usually built outside a city context. The world headquarters often takes the form of a very high skyscraper sitting plumb in the middle of a major city.

3. K. T. Gibbs, *Business Architectural Imagery in America 1870–1930* (Ann Arbor: University of Michigan Press, 1985).

4. R. Yee and K. Gustafson, *Corporate Design: The Interior and Architecture of Corporate America* (New York: Interior Design Books, 1983), 14–15.

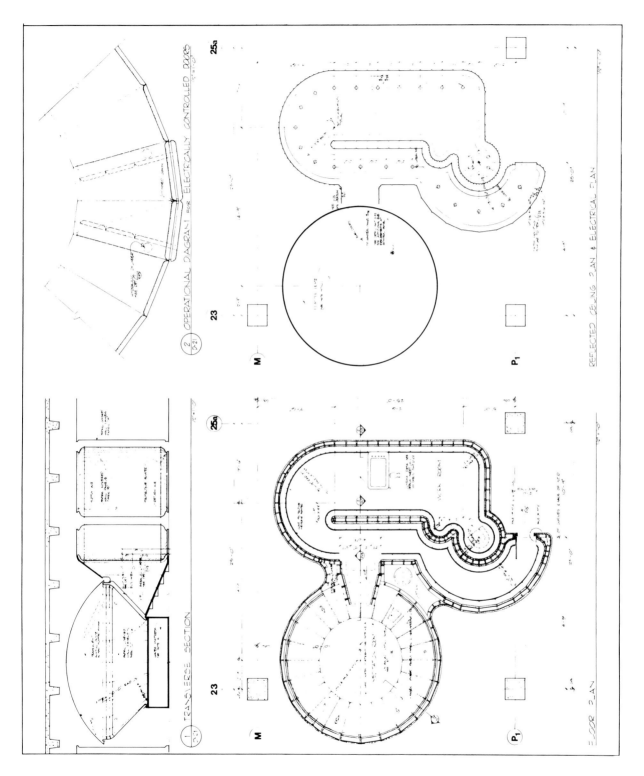

McDonald's headquarters: think tank, plans, section, and, details, Chicago, 1973, Associated Space Design.

5. The terms are in quotes for a specific reason: to indicate the artificiality, the test-tube construction. The "society" created by a corporation is, in fact, an artificial society that has been thought out, planned, and constructed by the leadership with a precise aim: the success of the corporation. This implies its constant and infinite growth. The task of the corporation leadership is astounding, to say the least. For more on this subject, see Peters and Waterman, *In Search of Excellence* (New York: Harper & Row, 1982), 81–86.

6. Peters and Waterman, xxii.

7. A. Fallucchi, "Corning Glass Design Spurs Engineers' Creativity," *Facilities Design & Management, for Corporate Executives, Managers and Planners of Office Environments,* January 1982.

8. Peters and Waterman, 122.

9. B. F. Skinner, *Science and Human Behavior* (New York: Macmillan, 1953).

10. A significant example of this is the Think Tank built at the MacDonald's headquarters in Chicago in 1973. It was the result of a collaboration between the interior designers and the space planners of Associated Space Design Incorporated of Atlanta, and the psychologists R. Thomson Putney and Thomas J. Erwin of the Department of Psychology of Georgia State University (see "The Thinking behind the Think Tank," *Modern Office Procedures,* May 1973). Another example is provided by the W. C. Decker Engineering Building, the outcome of a collaboration between the architects of Davis, Brody & Associates of New York and Dr. Thomas J. Allen, psychologist and researcher at the Massachusetts Institute of Technology Sloan School of Management (see "A Meeting of the Minds at Corning," *Architectural Record,* September 1981, and Faccucchi, "Corning Glass Spurs Engineers' Creativity").

11. Yee and Gustafson, 59.

12. Peters and Waterman, 80:

Psychologists study the need for self-determination in a field called "illusion of control." Stated simply, its findings indicate that if people think they have modest personal control over their destinies, they will persist at tasks. They will do better at them. They will become more committed to them. Now, one of the most active areas of this experimentation is the study of cognitive biases. The typical experiment here has subjects estimate their probability of success at future tasks after they have had some experience doing the same sort of activity. The results are pretty consistent: whether the subjects are adults or college sophomores, they overestimate the odds of succeeding at an easy task and underestimate the odds of succeeding at a hard one. In short, they regularly distort estimates of the possibilities of events . . . We need to succeed and stick out—desperately—so we overestimate the possibility of doing the easy task. And to preserve face and ensure security, we underestimate the possibility of getting the difficult task done.

Yee and Gustafson, 45–46:

The employee who perceives himself as having no control over his work area will generally feel he has no control over his work and certainly no control over others. For this reason, some designers are involving their client's staff in certain design choices. The choice could be small—such as do you want a pencil tray or no pencil tray in your drawer? Or on which side of the desk would you like your drawer pedestal? Helping to determine the environment of the company helps the employee to identify with the company.

13. *Ibid.*

14. Peters and Waterman, 51, 134.

15. E. Kohn, "Architecture, Interior and Industrial Design," *Leaders*, April–June 1983, 117–18.

16. Peters and Waterman, 79.

17. Yee and Gustafson, 46.

18. *Ibid.*, 83.

19. "The Thinking behind the Think Tank," *Modern Office Procedures*, Penton Publishing, © May 1973.

Index